SPIRITUAL TERRORISM

Fred DeRuvo

Spiritual Terrorism

Copyright © 2010 by Study-Grow-Know

All rights reserved. Written permission must be secured from the publisher to use or reproduce any part of this book, except brief quotations in critical reviews or articles.

Published in Scotts Valley, California, by Study-Grow-Know
www.studygrowknow.com • www.adroitpublications.com

Scripture quotations unless otherwise noted, are from The Holy Bible, King James Version. This version is in the public domain.

Images used in this publication (unless otherwise noted) are from clipartconnection.com and used with permission, ©2007 JUPITERIMAGES, and its licensors. All rights reserved.

Any Woodcuts used herein are in the Public Domain and free of copyright.

All Figure illustrations used in this book were created by the author and protected under copyright laws, © 2010, unless otherwise noted.

Additional research and assistance: Marie Swanson

Cover Design and Interior Layout: Fred DeRuvo

Library of Congress Cataloging-in-Publication Data

DeRuvo, Fred, 1957 –

ISBN 0982644353
EAN-13 9780982644355

1. Religion – Demonology & Satanism

Spiritual Terrorism

Contents

Foreword: 5
    Chapter 1: Terrorism from the Spiritual Realm 7
    Chapter 2: Walks-Ins, Apples and Fillers 14
    Chapter 3: Seth Spoke 48
    Chapter 4: Archangel Michael 58
    Chapter 5: Kryon of the Magnetic Service 64
    Chapter 6: Their Reality and Purpose 79
    Chapter 7: Their Deception 97
    Chapter 8: Last Days Are Here 109
    Chapter 9: Behind the Veil 130
Resources for Your Library 134

For such are false apostles, deceitful workers, transforming themselves into the apostles of Christ. And no marvel; for Satan himself is transformed into an angel of light. Therefore it is no great thing if his ministers also be transformed as the ministers of righteousness; whose end shall be according to their works.

– 2 Corinthians 11:13-15 (KJV)

FOREWORD

I was not intending to write another book that deals with the spiritual realm of demons. That is, until I received a few emails from a woman named Marie Swanson.

Marie shared how much she appreciated my books and then told me a bit about her background. It was interesting to realize how much God has used this woman to thwart the powers of darkness. By thwarting I mean she *exposed* them and their works, just as we are exhorted to do in Scripture (cf. Ephesians 5:11).

In the course of her adult life, she has seen much, experienced much, and helped much. Some of the things she has previously been involved in are wrong (and she is the first to admit it). Nonetheless, the insight she gained from those experiences gave her a firsthand understanding of how Satan works. They provided her with a clearer comprehension of the deceptions he frequently employs to accomplish his purposes.

Unbeknownst to Marie, the Lord seemed to be piquing my interest in some of the same areas. Even though I have published two books previously on the subject, there was more to write. One of the books I was reading at the time was by Brannon Howse titled, *Grave Influences: 21 Radicals and Their Worldviews That Rule America from the Grave.* A fascinating book that puts together in one package the histories of many of the individuals that, by themselves may not have accomplished much, but as Satan used them (under God's watchful eye), connecting one to the other, it became very clear that an extremely diabolical scheme has been in the making for quite some time.

The reality is that Howse's book forced me to consider anew the reality of the spiritual realm, and Satan as the prince of the power of the air. Though fully defeated, he obviously retains power and ability, which he uses in his attempts to thwart God's plans and create a world in which he is the ruler, not God.

It was about that time that Marie wrote asking if I had ever heard of "Walk-ins." I could not say I had, so I modified my search to include that area.

This then led to other areas of research in the demonic realm, in which Satan's minions take on every form of masquerade in order to deceive. It boggles the mind when considering just how massive and complex in scope the level of deception foisted upon humanity. Too many individuals are completely unaware of Satan's subterfuge tactics and go blissfully along believing that what they experience must be correct due to their spiritual bliss. If not corrected, they will unfortunately find that what they thought was bliss, was nothing more than a front, with hideously raw evil lurking just beyond reach and out of sight.

This book was written simply because it needs to be. With Marie's permission, tremendous research, and blessing, I have used a great deal of information she has gathered in her years of research. It is my prayer that her information will reveal the true sense of evil that is growing exponentially throughout the world today. I pray that if you are caught up in it, you will see it for what it is and do everything you can to run from it, by calling on the Name of Jesus Christ!

God is here to help. He loves you and He wants you free from the tyranny of Satan's lies, deceit, and grip. I pray that you will see the truth that is only found in Jesus Christ and embrace it. May God be with you and bless you.

Fred DeRuvo, June 2010

Chapter 1
Terrorism from the Spiritual Realm

We hear a great deal about terrorism today. The world has changed drastically over the past few years. The subject of terrorism or terrorists appears in the headlines of newspapers across the globe and the results are shown on TV and the Internet daily.

Though discussed here in the United States, terrorism was *their* problem, on the other side of the world. It was not something we personally experienced. Of course, that all changed with 9/11, when terrorism reared its ugly head within the borders of this country. Thousands died that day and our world forever changed.

War on Terrorism

The war rages on against those involved in terrorism. However, in all likelihood, this war will never be won. It may abate and may actually seem to go away for a while, but it will remain in one form or another, until Jesus returns.

This present administration has spent much time reaching out to the Muslim world. In some cases, under President Obama's leadership, the United States is now holding hands with countries that were previously declared terrorist strongholds. Beyond this, several organizations like United Nations Alliance of Civilizations and the U.N. Human Rights Commission. This would not be bad, except that both of these organizations are heavily anti-Israel.

When President Obama was running for election, he constantly intoned the words "change is coming." He never definitively stated what this particular change *meant*, and it was left up to the individual voter to decide. Many decided it meant change for the better and in their own minds they attached their details to Obama's mantra that allowed them to believe he had this country's best interests at heart.

Such has not been the case. Beyond President Obama's move toward obvious terrorist regimes and strongholds, he has pushed for a healthcare that includes all people, much to the chagrin of the taxpayers who will have to foot the bill.

President Obama has also circled the globe, literally *bowing* to Muslim leaders and others, as if the position of the president of the United States is somehow *beneath* them, or *subservient*. In his willingness to kowtow, other leaders see him as *weak*. Obama seems unwilling to use the military to defend our country even if nuclear arms are used against us here, further endorsing his weakness.

President Obama's position in favor of the illegal alien and undocumented worker has also become obvious. Referring to illegal immigrants recently as "visitors" from Mexico, he refuses to acknowledge that they are here *illegally*, without passport or permission. All of this is troubling to many of us, yet it continues unabated. President Obama has the ability to ignore others as no other president before him it seems.

I bring this to the fore not to complain about President Obama, but to highlight the fact that there is a good deal of activity in the spiritual realm that affects us. Demons, powerful and not so powerful, have been involved in bringing their master's plans to fruition. Of course, we know that none of his plans can even begin to come to the fore unless permitted by God Almighty (and Satan knows that as well). In spite of this, it is incumbent upon each authentic Christian to understand how Satan is working and what his goals are at each stage.

Some argue that we only need to know God's Word and that provides enough ammo against the enemy. Obviously, we need God and His Word. Without it, we are hopelessly lost and defeated.

It is also helpful to know our opponents game plan as well. Yes, this is outlined in God's Word, but we can also see it in the lives of people around us. In this way, we come to understand that the problem lies with the beings *behind* the people, not the people themselves.

Since President Obama has taken office, I do not necessarily feel more secure from terrorists. I do not believe this country is safer, nor do I believe that Americans traveling abroad are safer. In fact, I believe because of this administration's present policies, the United States is being forced under the bus. In essence, it appears that our current leadership has the goal of converting this republic into a Socialist regime. For that to happen, the Constitution of the United States would have to be set aside and with all the talk of a new world order, countries like the United States will be seen as antiquated.

The word "terrorism" has three meanings:

1. the use of violence and threats to intimidate or coerce, esp. for political purposes.
2. the state of fear and submission produced by terrorism or terrorization.
3. a terroristic method of governing or of resisting a government.[1]

In the countries where terrorism reigns, people live in a constant state of fear and intimidation. They never know when a bomb will go off, or a rocket will destroy. Everyone who carries a backpack, or who is dressed in a long overcoat in spite of the temperature is eyed with suspicion. Life is short and could end for anyone in these countries at any point in time.

In essence, life is short here in America as well. None of us knows the day or hour of our death. We simply live with a different attitude and demeanor because we do not constantly look death in the face.

Even when terrorists do nothing, people continue to live in fear of them doing something. This is no way to live and certainly, things are only going to worsen.

For Allah!
Recently, Faisal Shahzad, a Pakistan-born U.S. citizen, was arrested for allegedly planting an SUV laden with bombs in New York City's Times Square. Since his arrest, at least four others have been arrested. Frankly, I am surprised it has taken this long for these attempted acts of terrorism to occur within our own borders.

Timothy McVeigh was a homegrown terrorist as was the Unabomber. These individuals are *rare*, yet they too devastate. It appears though that within the ranks of Islam, there are *many* who are not only *will-*

---

[1] http://dictionary.reference.com/browse/terrorism

ing to give up *their* life for Allah, but are lining up to do just that. If they can take as many infidels (unbelievers in Islam) with them into the next life, all the better for them. Allah will be pleased and they will enter into their eternal rest of paradise, this according to Islam.

Terrorists do nothing but *destroy*. That is their sole intent. They live for that opportunity to kill or maim. They believe that through violence, Allah will be appeased and satisfied. They believe it is their responsibility to fight *for* Allah and they take that view seriously. One can only wonder why Allah is not able to defend himself. The God of the Bible says He will repay. He does not want or encourage His children to do that on His behalf.

It is one thing to understand how human beings as terrorists work to bring about the anarchy and chaos that they yearn to bring about, all so that the final Mahdi or Imam will appear to the world. With him comes peace through Islam, as he lays down Sharia Law throughout the globe. Sharia Law has no pity for anyone. There is no mercy and many times, there is no trial. It is essentially mob rule by mob mentality.

War on Spiritual Terrorism
Within the spiritual realm, *terrorism* exists there as well. This spiritual terrorism is much the same as that within the human realm. Multitudes of demons have one goal, to serve their master and do things for him and in his name. Through their spiritual terror cells, they wreak havoc on God's Creation through the very humans that God Himself has created.

While we see the physical terrorist, through pictures and video and sometimes, too close to home, we do *not* see the spiritual forces that terrorize the world's populace. While we are and should be concerned with the *physical* terrorists living among us, we should be far more concerned with the *spiritual* terrorists that walk among us who are *unseen* yet create far more mayhem.

These terrorists from the spiritual realm hate us, want nothing more than to destroy us, and the only thing that stops them from annihilating all humanity is God. Just as we need to understand how human terrorists think and act, we also need to be aware of the devil's schemes (cf. 2 Corinthians 2:11; 11:3; see also Ephesians 4:14; 6:11; 1 Peter 5:8). We are commanded to be alert to the wiles of the devil. Of course, we cannot fight him in our own strength, but God within us provides the consistency to stand *for* the truth, against Satan's lies.

Throughout this book, we will be looking at how demons from their spiritual realm, *collide* with, *affect*, and *infect* human beings in this realm. We must be aware of these realities in order that we will understand how the devil's schemes work and what he is attempting to accomplish. We are to be wise as serpents and gentle as doves (cf. Matthew 10:16). We are to *know* and with that knowledge, teach others, literally pulling them from the fire.

People do *not* want to be the target of terrorists. No one wants to be blown to bits. No one wants to die violently by some fanatic who earnestly believes that their deity sanctions acts of murder. Terrorism has taken on new meaning in today's world and because of it we are more and more on our guard and rightly so.

However, since terrorism in this human, physical realm does not happen without the intrusion of beings from the spiritual realm, then it is infinitely more important to understand their dealings with fallen humanity. We need to know how they snare their victims and once snared how they work through them to accomplish their master's bidding.

Knowledge and awareness produce the type of Christian that God can use. Christians are not here to sit in the back of the bus, doing nothing when a fight breaks out in the front. We are to be on our guard, making the most of every opportunity in the hopes of helping to free some souls from the powerful grip of darkness. This can only take place with Christians who have forsaken all to follow Christ. It is giving up all that we have (including any 'rights' to our own life), that Christ is able to work in and through us.

Many individuals are currently used by the devil and his cohorts, and need to hear the salvation message. Authentic believers need to be the ones who bring it to them. Are you willing?

Chapter 2
Walk-ins, Apples & Fillers

"Walk-ins" Moving in to Take Over

When I saw the movie *The Matrix,* I felt pretty certain that I knew where the Wachowskis were heading with it. In the movie, the main character Thomas A. Anderson, a computer hacker, played by Keanu Reeves, is told that he is Neo, *"the one"* who will apparently save the world from the Matrix. The Matrix is nothing more than a cleverly concealed complex system set up by machines in order to keep humans lulled into apathy.

The machines need the energy that humans produce in order to exist. To accomplish this, the machines created huge warehouses where human beings exist in the fetal position while immersed into a substance that gives them the nutrients they need. These humans are perpetually asleep, or in a dream state. The unfortunate part is that their dream state is so real that to them it is their reality and unbeknownst to them, it is merely a fabricated *façade*.

Neo's life became duller by the day, with the routine of it slowly killing him. He winds up meeting another character named Morpheus who tells him that he exists in a dream world, but has the opportunity to escape it. All he has to do is decide if he wants the blue or the red pill. One will put him back into his perpetual sleep and what happened to him will seem like a dream. The other will permanently pull him out of his dream state in order that he will be free to create his own reality.

He of course decides to take the pill that frees him from the Matrix (otherwise it would have been a very short movie), and thus begins the process of learning the ropes of his newfound freedom. He learns to manipulate what appears to be real for his advantage. Eventually, he overcomes and toward the end of the movie, turns to the audience and states that we can all create our own reality. It is up to us.

This theme – *creating our own reality* – has been with us forever it seems. Whether in movies, TV shows, books, articles, or something else, the idea has literally been pounded into us that we are the captains of our own fate.

Even a favorite trilogy – *Back to the Future* – ends with Doc Brown telling Marty that the future has not been written yet. It's yours to create. That concept is initially very freeing for many people. It provides a sense of relief on one hand, and pride on the other. When people stop to consider the ramifications of believing that each individual has the ability to create their own reality, it becomes quite a heady experience. What people of course fail to realize is that the phrase "creating your own reality" is merely code for telling yourself that each person is his or her own god. There is no higher authority for anyone except that individual.

All of this plays nicely with the New Age because they are all busy attempting to unlock their own deity within, which they believe will help them do what Neo says we should do. Instead of simply being dictated to, we should be the ones to dictate to ourselves.

Self-Actualization by Any Other Name
The entire process of New Age thought can likely be summed up in one concept: *ascending to the highest possible plane through self-effort.* You see, according to New Age proponents, over eons of evolution, humanity has grown to the point of *self-awareness*. This is what separates us from the animals that live instinctively, but do not necessarily have a self-awareness as we humans enjoy.

While elf-awareness wakes us up from our spiritual slumber it has, *we are told*, gotten us to the point of merely realizing that we have not yet arrived. There is much more growth ahead of us and if we are to rise to the levels before us, we must endeavor to do so by using what we have learned through self-awareness. We must persist in unlocking our own intrinsic deity, as Jesus did, as Muhammad did, as Gandhi did, along with many others. This is the theology of the New Age movement.

Fortunately, for humanity, we are not alone, left to our own devices. There are others and they are here – they tell us – to help us achieve the state for which we have been created. That state is the state of *self-actualization*, which is merely another way of saying that we *recognizing our deity*, and then beginning the long process of relying on it, listening to it, and growing from it. This is a very simplistic explanation and one thing that the New Age is *not*, is simplistic. It is purposefully complex and oftentimes confusing so that it has an air of *high level intelligence* to it.

The New Age is not for idiots, although they can benefit as well, but certainly not to the degree that the intelligent individual will benefit. The person who is able to *self-actualize* through *self-awareness*, gains much. In essence, the secrets of the universe begin to open up to him or her. The darkness begins to turn to *light*. Once this light begins to dawn, the individual recognizes that they have encountered deity, and that deity is within their very souls already.

Many within the New Age believe themselves to be what are called "starseeds." These are entities that have allegedly planted themselves within or near (at first) the body of a human being. Once they receive an invitation from the human, they begin the process of entering and eventually taking total control. It may take years for the person to realize who they are in reality, or it may take a much shorter period of time. It all depends on the person and their situation.

Many of the books written by top New Agers are written *by* and *to* people who have already become self-aware of some type of deity within himself or herself. This self-revelation or awareness allows them to become more and more familiar with their true identity. One article states, *"The unfoldment of the wonderment of the New Age continues. You who are starseed are being affected more at this time because the process of preparation must be completed prior to the major cleansing and purging activities. Why is this? Because starseed will play a signifcant part in the assistance of the planet's transformation. Therefore they must be readied, they must be trained, they must be prepared, and their star qualities and capabilities must be opened and released in order to do the work that must be done to accomplish their mission. You know this is happening at this time because so many of you are experiencing changes occurring at different levels. Yes, this process is somewhat confusing and somewhat uncomfortable."*[2]

The newsletter article just quoted is summing up what might be described as the *new birth* within the starseed. Within this newsletter just referenced, there are additional messages from beings named *Commander Apollo (Delos Command), Lord Sananda, Kryos, Christmon* and *Dream Singer.* These messages include explanations related to some of the *opportunities for change, how to discern messages, focusing, learning to fly in the spiritual realm,* and *to trust the spirit within enough to let go* and let the entity *control.*

Looks Like Christianity and Sounds Like Christianity
Of course, what is fascinating is that in many examples provided, they read like Christianity, much as learning to hear and follow the nudging of the Holy Spirit, for instance. At one point, an article states, *"The chances are that if you feel safe and secure in your present job, you will not even be looking for another opportunity for employment. So you stay in your safe and secure but dull job and continue to waste your God given talents. No change, no gain. Now let's say that the Creator says: 'Alright, if you will not move, I will assist you with a little nudge.' One day your boss says, 'Sorry, my friend, but business is slow and you've got to go.' The thought of suddenly having to leave your comfortable job of nine years sends feelings of terror through your consciousness. You must close the door behind you before you are aware of the wonderful opportunity that may await behind yet another closed door."*[3]

What has just been described could have been one Christian talking to another. In fact, as I write this, a situation has cropped up in my life from out of nowhere in which it appears that God has shut one door very tightly and opened another.

---
[2] From a newsletter produced by Universalia, Denver, CO
[3] Ibid

The difference of course, is that this author is a Christian, and the God of the universe *guides* my steps. I have been bought with the price of Jesus' blood and I am His *forever*. He guides me. He brings things to fruition in and through me. He is the one to whom all glory and honor goes because He and He alone knows what is best for me in this life.

To the New Ager, outwardly this process may *appear* to be the same process that Christians go through, with one major exception. While New Agers ultimately worship themselves, the god they *believe* to be them, is none other than Satan or one of his many messengers of death. Since we know that Satan is an imitator and that he often comes as a messenger or angel of light (*"And no marvel; for Satan himself is transformed into an angel of light,"* 2 Corinthians 11:15), then it also follows that he would design his oversight of those who inadvertently worship him to appear to mirror the Christian's experience. That is a no-brainer.

Since to the New Ager, *god is in all and through all*, it is at this point when these self-actualized individuals come to realize that their deity is merely part of the large, overarching, all-inclusive deity that comprises all things and all people. It should not at all be difficult to see how such an experience would feel to those who believe they have found the key to unlock the door to that spiritual world of self-realized deity.

As stated, there are myriads of entities among us from their spiritual realm that offer their "help" to us. Presented as benevolent, kind, and altruistic, these beings say they are from other worlds and have come here out of the kindness of their own hearts and love for all human beings. Of course, they have something to gain from it as well, since many of them also tell us that either they or some group connected with them is our actual creator, *not* the God of the Bible.

These entities surround themselves with light and the humans who *willingly* encounter them, often experience heights of joy and happiness they say they never found in any religious setting. They believe that they have finally found what they have been looking for and their *feelings* provide the proof, which is all they need.

It's the Same Message with Different Words
Within the full scope, complexities of UFO study, and research, it has become clear to many that the message across the board appears to be one in the same. We have reported some of this in prior books, but it bears repeating that it does not matter what particular entity is speaking, because they all essentially speak about the same thing. *"Our purpose in coming at this time is to help speed up these reactions so you will be prepared for the change-over in the Earth's frequency. This is taking place over a number of years. Many of your people are being affected mentally and spiritually in a discomforting way, and some of them in a very spiritual way."*[4]

We are told that the earth will undergo a tremendous shift in its *frequency*. This, along with a good deal of techno-speak, sounds *scientific*. In fact, who would argue that these messages should not be taken as true? This coming change in frequency is described differently by other beings, however, the same event is meant.

"The program that is in operation is to prepare the Earth for a major rise in consciousness, to what you call Christ awareness but what we term communication with Universal Energy."[5] I don't mean to sound sarcastic, but can you imagine these demons sitting around coming up with this stuff? One says, *"Let's call it 'Universal Energy' because it'll sound more impressive and take them further away from the truth that there is only one God and that He is Victor!"* and they all give a rousing cheer in agreement!

---

[4] Nada-Yolanda, *op. cit.*, p 65
[5] Ibid, p 25

Spiritual Terrorism

The more I study this entire area, the more convinced I am that many paranormal stories authored by now famous individuals, which are allegedly *fiction*, are dictated in some manner to the author of that book, whether through dreams, voices, or meditations. Many of those books are turned into movies to the delight of Sci-Fi and horror fans everywhere. How are writers of these Sci-Fi, horror, and paranormal able to write as many best-selling books that eventually turn into blockbuster movies as they do? I can think of only one way. For the most part, the messages of those books and movies are always the same.

The messages found within these books and movies have been used to indoctrinate people for generations. What at first was seen as something so unbelievable that it could not be real, has come to the point of being *lovingly* accepted by most throughout the world.

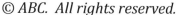

© *ABC. All rights reserved.*

Satan's Efforts in Redirection
Satan knows what he is doing. For those who have interests *in* and proclivities *toward* the spiritual, his goal is to *redirect* them *away* from God *to* himself, a false god. He does this in any number of ways, but largely through the auspices of the New Age movement, simply because it has so many different branches and beliefs that there is something for everyone. Crystal power? Tarot? Psychics? Anything that someone thinks he or she needs, Satan can provide.

The only other groups he needs to contend with are those who are geared much more toward the belief that no God exists at all, *atheists*, *agnostics*, and *skeptics*. He needs to keep these people away from any source that might cause them to question their own belief that God does not exist, or worse, sources that open their eyes to the truth!

Both of the above groups – religious and non - can gain from and appreciate the genres of the paranormal, Sci-Fi, and horror. While the former often sees truth within these types of entertainment, the latter views it mainly for amusement. Of course, both groups are being collectively deceived and reprogrammed in their thinking by the enemy.

Consider the many books and movies that have been around for the past 50 or 60 years. More and more of them mix horror with the paranormal, or Sci-Fi with the paranormal, or all three. When I was growing up, the horror movies were the old Universal *Frankenstein*, *Dracula*, and *Mummy* movies. There were simply scary movies where something supernatural or extraordinary occurred to the main character in the movie. Because it was not generally believed that these things could actually happen, we did not put too much stock in it, though we probably should have because of the Pandora's Box these movies opened to society.

How about *Dark Shadows*? This was the first daytime soap opera to deal in the supernatural and paranormal, beginning in 1966. The

Spiritual Terrorism

main character, Barnabas Collins, was a *vampire*. The series itself was apparently *based on a dream* that creator Dan Curtis had, about a girl who took a long train ride and wound up at a large mansion.

For the series, the girl was known as Victoria Collins and over the course of the show, werewolves, zombies and other paranormal type characters popped up.[6] Interestingly, Curtis came up with the idea from a *dream* he had. I have often thought that when we dream, we are not only closest to death, but our mind is much more open to attack and suggestion. It is important to be in prayer daily that God would protect our hearts and minds even as we sleep.

Many ideas for horror, Sci-Fi, and paranormal books, TV series, and movies came to fruition out of someone's dream (nightmare?). Who can forget other hit movies like Clive Barker's *Hellraiser* series, or

Gosh, who wouldn't want a Hellraiser action figure?

©Cinemarque Entertainment. All rights reserved.

---

[6] http://en.wikipedia.org/wiki/Dark_Shadows

Friday, the 13th, or *Halloween*, or even *Freddy Krueger*? These movies and characters are icons within these genres and well known to millions. All of these things serve to downplay our fears about the unknown. They also serve to recreate within us a new understanding of the paranormal.

Interestingly enough, when a movie like *Mars Attack!* comes along, it is so campy (purposefully) that we sit and laugh at the zaniness on the screen. The Martians look weird, sound weird, and are generally over the top, along with the human characters in the movie. Even here though, while we *know* that this is silly camp, because we laugh at it, we melt more of any residual fears within us related to aliens and the paranormal.

Another series of movies that became a hit is based on a comic book. The Men in Black (M.I.B.) franchise centers around the idea that aliens live among us. For the most part, they have adopted human-looking bodies. Every so often, something goes wrong and their cov-

©Columbia Tristar and Amblin Entertainment. All rights reserved.

er is blown. Actual human beings, who were not aware of their presence, get a peek behind the masquerade. This won't do, so the Men in Black step in to clean up the mess and erase memories so that human beings can continue to live in this world unknowingly among aliens.

We have become acclimated to the ideas of *spiritual entities, aliens* from various planets and solar systems, and even *enlightened beings* or *ascended masters*. It is part of our culture. We accept their presence, whereas before, we only accepted the *idea* that they might exist. Now, for many, it is a foregone conclusion.

Nevertheless, how do these entities *move* among us? Moreover, how do they provide information *to* us? How do people *know* that they are benevolent, as opposed to malevolent? Can we know for sure?

Walk-Ins
Walk-ins have many names. Whether they are called *Walk-ins, Starseeds, Wanderers, Apples, Fillers*, or something else entirely, their purpose is essentially the same. Allegedly, they come *into* a person's body, taking up residence, as the person's previous spirit *exits* for one reason or another. It is said this usually occurs during some traumatic time in the person's life, like a near death experience.

On the Spirit Library Web site, an individual names *Shekina* (note the misspelling of the biblical word "Shechinah" here), provides this information regarding *Blue Ray Beings* (in September of 2008): "*As a Blue Ray Being, you came to transform the damaged, mutated DNA of humanity, and set the stage for the other rays to come. You were not recognized for your unique divine light and had to recognize yourselves. It was tricky spiritual business as you were super sensitive beings, though you had the spiritual power tools to be victories in your mission. For the last 100 years the Indigos, Rainbows, Crystals and you, the Blue Rays, have been incarnating to create a vibrational shift to the higher dimensions. You the Blue Ray Beings are the overlooked and forgotten ones, and have been essential in clearing and setting the stage for humanities ascension. Because of you, Blue Ray Beings, earth will be able to take her rightful place in the galactic and universal councils of oneness and peace.*

"We Wish to 'Thank you', from the ones that can't articulate your divine presence, all of humanity, your star sisters and brothers of light and the sacred higher realms. We are in constant praise and support of you"!

"Remember! Blue Ray, there is much more coming for you Divine changes Your time has come."[7]

Many guides, teachers, and those who channel within the New Age define a type of hierarchy within the spiritual realm from where these entities originate. Notice though that in the above quote, the emphasis is on a coming *vibrational shift*, which is merely another name for *higher consciousness*, or *frequency shift*.

According to this same Web site, the mission of the Blue Ray Being is simple, but also very essential. It is to *"Infiltrate the system in a normal capacity, always remembering who you are and where you came from,* **planting the seeds of peace, love, light and higher awareness**. *No matter how painful, long or arduous the job was, it was your mission and you had the spiritual tools, insight and divine light to see it through."*[8] (emphasis added)

Shekina finishes with this tantalizing tidbit: *"In the next transmission - Blue Ray update 'Finally Big changes for the Blue Rays' and what to expect as we near 2012".*[9] Most know of the Mayan calendar and the fact that it ends on December 21, 2012. Because of this and other things, the year 2012 has become a big event long before it arrives,

---

[7] http://spiritlibrary.com/forum/discussions/channeled-messages-and-articles/are-you-from-the-blue-ray-star-beings-walk-ins-the
[8] http://spiritlibrary.com/forum/discussions/channeled-messages-and-articles/are-you-from-the-blue-ray-star-beings-walk-ins-the
[9] Ibid

much like Y2K. People *anticipate* things to come and the excitement of expectation is building.

New Terminology

During the process of writing this book, I have been corresponding with Marie Swanson, who has done extensive research in this area. She said, *"Over the last several decades there has been a new terminology creeping into the different segments of our society, all of which seems to have a common thread...demons. Entities, Spirits, Walk-ins, Ancient Ones, Masters, E.T.s, etc., they are co-habitating or "soul trading"! These are some of the 'new' names most of which I was not familiar with until recently. In exchanging information [with another researcher], we found some very interesting incidents taking place. They were the names of these 'new' beings. The following names are: Fillers, Apples, Wanderers, Bridge-people, Star-people, Messengers, Walk-ins, Channelers, and Skin-walkers. These co-habitators or soul traders may take partial control, complete control, or total control!"*[10]

What is tacitly interesting here is that people *routinely* speak of these types of beings *as existing*. These are intelligent people discussing them and very few bat an eye, or cast doubt on the topic of the discussion. However, as Marie states, *"Today if you believe in a personal devil and possession you are looked upon as someone who is mentally ill. However, if you believe and accept a 35,000-year-old ENTITY from Atlantis who speaks through a human being you are looked upon as enlightened and broad minded. These human beings [with] whom they are co-habitating are looked upon as special, bordering on elite or super human or...CHOSEN! Now that frightens me! Hitler also believed in a new race, the Aryan race...a superior race, a new twist to an age old deception."*[11]

---

[10] Letter from Marie Swanson (on file)
[11] Ibid

Marie explains further some of the aspects of these beings, which set them apart. *"[facets] seem to interconnect with each other, either by the human, the entity or the combination of them together. They are as follows:*

1. *there are smells or odors that accompany most of these experiences. They are described as foul, rancid, putrid, disgusting, rotting, sulfur, matching burning to fragrances of flowers and the smell of roses.*
2. *The change of temperature, an unpleasant cold, a sudden drop of temperature, a cold spot or area*
3. *There are electrical failures, T.V. interference, cars stalling, lights going on and off, electrical shock*
4. *Sudden stillness, all noise ceases...frogs, crickets, dogs, cattle, birds and even other insects*
5. *Forgotten time, memory loss*
6. *The co-habitating with entities creates a change in personality*
7. *Desire to commit suicide, self-mutilate, kill, and go completely insane"*[12]

There have been many instances of these things happening and of course, Hollywood attempts to mirror them by including them in movies, which become blockbuster hits. *Close Encounters of the Third Kind*, was probably the first and most memorable, separating itself from the multitude of schlocky Sci-Fi movies that came before it, at least with respect to the subject of *alien* life. Another genre found in *The Exorcist* created havoc in movie theaters and afterwards because of the fear it generated of demons, the devil, and the paranormal.

Meditation is the Key
It seems to be the mission of all of these *beings*, in whatever form they present themselves, to force humanity to become fully open to their existence and presence in our dimension. This is mainly ac-

---
[12] Letter from Marie Swanson (on file)

complished through the art of *meditation*. This is so because through this process, the human being is *voluntarily* opening himself or herself up to the spatial dimension in which these entities exist. Because they are in essence, *invited* by human beings through meditative practices, they are perfectly free to *enter* into that person's life, or that person's body, or *both*.

The goal is that the more human beings there are who open themselves up to these entities, the more these entities will be able to do what they want to do *in* and *through* people, and to this *planet*. The real problem of course is that once a person opens the door of their mind to these beings, more than one can enter.

One Web site includes a note of warning regarding the choices that human beings make. *"As long as people, individually and as a whole, allow the problems of the world to fester,* **all people have to share in the karmic burden of taking turns living in the deplorable conditions that selfish behavior creates and sustains**,"[13] (emphasis added). We referenced this mindset in previous books showing a connection between this type of thinking and preparation for the coming Rapture of the Church and ultimately, the Tribulation period. The explanation of the coming Rapture will be clearly understood by those within the New Age. In essence, the Rapture event will offer *proof* to New Agers that the malcontents were removed from this planet, in order to allow further spiritual evolution.[14] This type of message has been transmitted to human channelers for the past 40 years or so and when it does occur, New Agers will be primed for it.

Malachi Martin reported in his book *Hostage to the Devil* that *"once [the person] voluntarily accepted it – and he insists today that he knew he was accepting some 'remote' or 'alien' control – he was suddenly in-*

---

[13] http://www.reunificationchurch.org/guidelines_for_sound_spiritual_concepts.htm
[14] For further information on the removal of non-New Agers from the earth, see author's previous works *Some of Satan's Major Lies Seen as Truth, The PreTrib Rapture, and A Deceptive Orthodoxy,* all available through online booksellers.

undated. He now felt as if serpentine thoughts were touching the furthest reaches of his mind, and that fine tendrils were closing around each fiber of his will."

Yearning for Total Control

It is obvious that these entities will not stop until they control every aspect of people and this planet. To that end, more people daily seem to be giving themselves over to a power resident within these entities that human beings know nothing about. These entities – or Starseeds – come to this planet under the guise of administering help to people and the planet overall. They assert that they want to assist in the development of the spiritual hierarchy in order that this planet and its citizens can evolve to the next spiritual plane. It certainly seems that while this is what they *say*, their intentions are far more egregious and *evil*.

This is something that Jacques Vallée concluded in his book *Messengers of Deception*. He stated, "*WHATEVER their origin, their purpose seems aimed at achieving social changes through psychological conditioning.*" Vallee came to believe that these beings *do* actually exist, *but* their purposes are fully *malevolent*, not beneficial to humanity.

So whatever people call them, it is clear that though they *profess* to come from other galaxies, or other planets within our galaxy, the truth of the matter may be far different. The term "Starseed" fits best, since they are here to *seed* themselves into and through human beings who live on this earth.

"Starseeds are individuals who exist here on the earth plane in a three dimensional human body, but whose soul may have originated from another planet, star system, galaxy, dimension or parallel universe. These inter-dimensional or extra-terrestrial souls have incarnated onto the earth plane and into the human body/vehicle through the normal process of birth but may or may not have the free will choice to be here. Most starseed souls are born into the human body/vehicle with no con-

scious knowledge of who they are, where they came from, or why they are here. Starseeds are usually sent here to complete a type of mission, or they may have personally chosen to be here for a specific purpose."[15]

The above definition is an interesting one. Whether you believe it to be real is *not* the point. Many people *do* accept it as truth and they *live* as if it is truth. More and more people throughout this world are coming to believe that we exist and live in *dimensions*. It is not so much that aliens come from other planets, but that they are increasingly believed to be *inter-dimensional*. As you sit and read this book, you exist in a particular dimension. However, right next to you, off to your left, but unable to be *seen* or *physically experienced*, is another dimension in which many entities hustle and bustle about. They can break through to our dimension, but we are not able to break through to theirs primarily because of the physical nature of our bodies.

This is also part of the Bible. Second Kings highlights this: *"And Elisha prayed, and said, LORD, I pray thee, open his eyes, that he may see. And the LORD opened the eyes of the young man; and he saw: and, behold, the mountain was full of horses and chariots of fire round about Elisha,"* (2 Kings 6:17).

What the young man saw after Elisha prayed was the spiritual realm behind the veil. There he saw God's army, yet they were invisible to him in the physical realm.

As human beings, we experience life within our own four dimensions of the universe:

1. length
2. height
3. width
4. time

---

[15] http://www.dimension1111.com/starseeds-and-walkins.html

Though time is primarily a *temporal* dimension, it is a dimension nonetheless that we are capable of *experiencing*. We age because of time. Essentially, for human beings, the universe that we experience is four dimensions, yet scientists are now arriving at the conclusion that there may be as many as ten dimensions. If so, six of them cannot be experienced by us. Yet something likely *does* exist in these other dimensions, so what is there?

Would They Lie?
The answer may be that other entities exist there. As mentioned, this seems to have been the belief of Jacques Vallée and others mentioned in my previous book *Demons in Disguise*. If this is true, then it is also likely true that they are *presenting* themselves to humanity as beings that are here to help us move up to the spiritual evolutionary planes above us. Everything written on the subject from the New Age perspective indicates this, yet no real substantial proof is offered as verification. We are left to either take these beings word for it, or not.

It can be somewhat complicated when discussing walk-ins because it reads like something right out of Star Trek, or some other Science Fiction genre. In fact, the more this entire area is studied, the more easily convinced a person becomes in seeing many connections between science fiction books and movies and the New Age and their beliefs.

The largest issue at stake today seems to be that people are chasing after *experiences* rather than God and His Word. Due to the fall of humanity, everything has been corrupted, including man's ability to *feel*. We cannot rely on feelings at all to help us make our decisions. It simply does not work. I am *not* referring to a sense where an authentic believer is led by the Holy Spirit (which normally comes with some way to confirm its authenticity). I am talking about how badly people in today's world want to *feel good*. To this end, they will chase after anything they believe will fill that empty space. However, this empty space was meant to be filled by God *only*. This is why the need to create a cleverly disguised substitute is necessary and this is where Satan excels.

If you consider many of the experiences related by those within the New Age movement or those who say they have been abducted by and met aliens, too often the experience appears to replicate something that a Christian might describe for the new birth. The feelings are often described as being totally good and even *glowing*, or *ecstatic*. It is not unusual for a tremendous sense of overwhelming "love" for others to begin to take shape within the individual. Sometimes, the initiate references a strong enveloping white light.

These individuals fully and firmly believe that they have met *the* God of the universe. More often than not though, these entities that come surrounded by *light*, are too quick to deny that Jesus Christ is God in the flesh. They refer to Him merely in terms of being an overall consciousness, not an authentic Person. This is one of the lies, which Paul rebutted in his letter to the Colossians. The people in Colossae were being force fed the Gnostic idea that Jesus had not really come in the flesh, but had been a *phantom* of sorts. He was merely representative of something greater. That same lie exists today and it is commonly repeated by the entities that claim to be here for our good.

Seth
The entire walk-in phenomenon largely became known through Jane Roberts, who channeled a being named Seth. Through Roberts, Seth revealed many things that he said take place in the spiritual realm, often between our spirits and other spirits. We are not necessarily aware that these things are happening, because we are normally too attuned to this physical realm.

For instance, Seth taught that a *walk-in* spirit might approach a person's human spirit if it sees that the person is depressed, or starting to hate life here on earth. It begins to communicate with that individual's spirit and eventually an agreement may be arrived at between the human spirit and the walk-in, in which the human spirit agrees to trade places with the walk-in. If a human being gets so depressed that he or she commits suicide, then that human's body is wasted. Since it is no longer alive, no soul or spirit can exist within it and the walk-in needs to find another spirit in another body willing to trade places. This process is often described as a very pragmatic negotiation that may go something like this:

"The Walk-In soul begins negotiations during the human's dream time, saying 'instead of your dying or committing suicide, which is a waste of a human body that could be used in service of the Light, please allow me to help. When you're ready, I'll take over your body, and you can go home to heaven with full honors. I'll feed your cat, help your children with their homework, call your mother every Sunday, and take care of your other responsibilities'."[16]

The problem of course, is because the walk-in does not possess the full personality of the original soul/spirit, when it trades places with that soul, the human may act strange, or evidence huge differences in personality. This is often how people learn an exchange has been made between spirits. A common indicator is when other people tell the person that they are not the same person anymore. They have changed. They seem *unrecognizable.*

So what is the purpose of this soul exchange beyond keeping a good physical body alive? In general, the walk-in's job is said to teach us human beings about *divine love*, *peace*, *happiness*, and things of that nature. Again though, where is the proof?

The world needs love and the world needs peace, to this, all would agree. The problem of course is that as we will see, this divine love and peace that the New Age is selling is far from God's definition. At best the New Age can only provide a facsimile and without being able

---

[16] http://talkingtoheaven.webs.com/walkins.htm

to compare it to God's love and peace, the human being has nothing else to go on, except what they are told (and feel) from the entities.

Through Jane Roberts and her spiritual mentor Seth, the world learned about this process of *soul exchange*. At that time, it was a mystery to a great degree and it seemed that largely, the norm was to exchange souls without the human host really being aware of the trade. With time, this has *changed*. Things are now done more in the open. Now, more individuals are stepping forward to claim that they have experienced soul exchange. They have had a walk-in. They know it and can attest to it because of the way they *feel*.

On another Web site, we read, "*There are many conscious walk-ins taking place now. The incoming soul is usually part of or from the same Oversoul monad*, and on rare occasions it can be a complete new monad. This is a soul that is aware of the Walk-in transfer and contract that is about to take place. There are usually very few or no veils with conscious Walk-ins, and it is always agreed with by both souls, and is by choice.*"[17] (*unit)

So we can see that as time has moved forward, the process of soul exchange has become more *obvious* and therefore, more *accepted* without question. Why this exchange is now discussed as normal, and no longer hidden from the individual human being will be discussed soon.

Since the mid to late 60s when Roberts first encountered Seth (using the Ouija board), others have *taken* the baton. Ruth Montgomery came later and claimed to have her own spirit guides, who provided her with a great deal of information from the spiritual realm.

One Web site claims that these walk-ins are here for one purpose, to move us into the *new world order*. Within the New Age movement, this is unifying belief that the world *needs* to move into a new world

---

[17] http://www.livewithlight.com/classes.php

order so that this planet and its inhabitants might graduate to the next spiritual level. Without this coming new world order, man as well as the earth, is sunk, without hope.

More Room to Work
What is needed here is solid *information*, not ideas based on *feeling*. Obviously, something is happening to many people, so what is it all about? Can we know? It seems clear that Satan is being given more room to work to accomplish his goals.

The Restrainer seems to be moving out of the way, little by little, until we will all arrive at the point when the Restrainer will move *completely* out of the way. At that point, all hell will literally break loose onto this planet. Preparations in the spiritual realm for this have been moving forward for years. Until then, things are gearing up for that time, with more leeway given to the enemy of our souls by more and more unsuspecting human beings who choose to believe these entities are what they say they are, but are *not*.

We have spoken of meditation before and most are aware that it is a major aspect of the New Age movement. Through meditation, the attempt is made to literally *empty* the mind. Once this is achieved, alpha wave patterns take over and the mind is literally put into neutral.

Because the mind is in neutral, it becomes extremely easy for the individual to become open to suggestion and even possession. Any spirit out there who wants to deceive is free to do so. The person meditating is unable to discern the truth of the matter. Are they hearing truth or lies? At that point, they can *only* go by what they *feel*. Unfortunately, feelings are not perfect or even good barometers for discernment. Feelings can be manufactured and the wool has been pulled over many people's eyes because of it.

Once a person enters a deep meditative state, they can easily succumb to whatever they are told or shown. If a spirit demon decides to say that it is Jesus Christ, how will the person know otherwise? They will not be able to discern it because their *feelings* will tell them that this spirit *is* who it says it is and that is all the person needs.

In the realm of the New Age movement, there are the *Seths*, the *Raphaels* (Barbara Marciniak's guide), and others with even more mundane names. However, there are also a fair share of spirits, who call themselves *Jesus*, or *Archangel Michael*, or *Gabriel*.

These spirits who claim to be these beings are never required by the human being who is being used as a channel, to prove their identities *to* the human beings they seek to *affect, infect, molest,* and *infest.* Because they bring to the person wonderful *feelings*, their *motives, character*, or *identities* are ever questioned. They are simply accepted for who they *claim* to be.

It is Difficult to Trust...in THIS World

In our physical world we expect to see people's *identification* all the time. We do not simply accept what we are told. We want proof. Why do we believe that things are different in the spiritual realm? If someone comes to the door saying they are someone, we want them to provide proof that they are who they say they are, and if they cannot, then we would likely quickly close the door and call the police.

In our world, we have learned not to take the word of someone simply because he or she says it. Go to the airport sometime and try to board a plane without proper I.D. You will not get far.

Try to apply for a passport without providing a legitimate birth certificate. You will not be able to apply. Apply for a credit card and see what happens if a credit check shows you have two social security cards assigned to you. All of these situations demand that we prove our identity.

Years ago, this was not as necessary because towns were smaller and people knew one another. Doors were often left unlocked because no one expected anyone to come in and rob them.

We have learned the hard way that many people cannot be trusted. In spite of the adage *innocent until proven guilty*, this is not how society acts. We *assume* guilt until the individual can prove they are not guilty. That is how much our world has changed over the past four or five decades.

Yet, when it comes to the spiritual realm, people believe that the entities there, would *never* attempt to pull the wool over our eyes. This is especially so considering the fact that the *feelings* that accompany such an experience are too good to be *evil*!

In our world, when people have relied on how they *feel* about something, they generally wind up getting into trouble. How many times have we read about a person who picked up a hitchhiker, or trusted a friendly face, only to discover that the friendly face quickly turned to something horrible? If the person survives the encounter, they might be heard saying something like "*I was slightly uneasy at first, but their smile reassured me.*"

When we *drive* our cars, most of us lock our doors. When we *park* our cars, we roll up the windows and lock the doors. Anything in plain sight might be moved to the trunk. We do this because we *assume* that there are car thieves around who are just waiting to see which car remains unlocked! We want it to be difficult for them.

When we leave our house in the morning, we lock our doors and windows. Many people own guns, or dogs, or both for protection. We spend time reinforcing windows and doors, maybe adding an alarm system to our car or home, or doing other things that make it difficult to break into, in the hopes that the burglar will go somewhere else.

In all these things, we take time to do everything we can to protect ourselves so that we will not fall prey to some criminal out wandering the streets looking for the perfect victim. We do not want to be the next crime statistic.

Yet, when it comes to beings in the *spiritual* realm, most believe that they are too altruistic to tell us lies. It is believed that evil spirits will *always* present themselves as unadulterated *evil* and no evil spirit would ever try to be seen as *good*. Why do we *assume* this? That is being way too gullible and goes against all sense and reason. However, this is what the average New Ager does, *daily*.

Walk-ins and Demons
Not long ago, I was listening to an audio capture of a pastor exorcising a woman who certainly seemed to be *possessed*. During the process, the demon within the woman began speaking *from* her. With a male voice, it called itself "the keeper" and "the guardian." Its job was to *stay* in *possession* of the woman's body.

As the pastor began praying, the demon started to manifest itself even more, arguing with the pastor. The demon also began making *animal* noises along with mechanical or machine-like noises. When the pastor spoke of the *blood* of Christ, the demon could not contain itself, *growling* at the mention of it. Eventually, as the pastor spoke directly to the demon, rebuking it in the Name of Jesus Christ, the demon began to argue, saying that it *"had the right to be"* in the woman's body.

The stated goal of the demon was to "terminate" the woman, so that she would spend eternity with all demons. In fact, the demon specifically stated *"**we** will do everything we can to terminate her."* It was clear that this demon was working in concert with *other* demons.

The demon stated that it was *"sent here to guide her, to protect her, and to lead her."* When the pastor told the demon that Jesus Christ had come to die for her, the response from the demon was "*she has not yet made that choice.*" When the pastor told the demon that it was a miracle that the woman had contacted him, the demon's response was "*someone out there was praying for her.*"

The pastor then indicated that the demon's hour of controlling this woman was over. The demon again countered with "*I have a right to be here.*" When asked what that right was, the reply was "*she is not yet accepting your God.*"

Interestingly enough, the demon also claimed that it, along with hundreds of other demons had inhabited this woman through *generational* contact, *transference*, and *possession* through many relatives before her. When the woman began to pray, the demon attempted to interrupt her whenever she tried to speak the Name of Jesus.

The most eye-opening parts of the audio are when the pastor asked the demon three questions:

1. Is Jesus Christ Lord?
2. Is Satan defeated?
3. Did Jesus Christ rise from the dead?

To *all three* questions, the demon is heard *sullenly* and *quietly* admitting, "yes," (while sounding like a snake; yesssss). Just prior to answering the third question, it sounded like the demon was spitting and growling at the same time, yet, it answered in the *affirmative*.

Now, whether this audio is genuine is difficult to determine. It certainly *sounded* real and it is easy to imagine a demon responding the way this one responded. What other choice do they have? The reality is that demons *know* they are defeated. They *know* that Jesus is Lord. They understand that the *resurrection of Jesus Christ* sealed their master's (Satan), and their defeat.

So why do they continue to do Satan's bidding? It is very likely that if they fail to continue, he could bind them in a prison made for them. Their decision to continue to serve him keeps them from incarceration until that time when God carries out the sentence that the resurrection of Jesus Christ wrought. Not only that, but it is clear that they want to bring as many human souls into hell with them as possible.

Defeated

Whether Satan is defeated or not, he continues to act as though he has *not* been defeated. He is putting all of his energy and effort into destroying God's plans and purposes as well as the very Creation that came into being (including Satan himself!) by God Almighty. Though fully defeated, he will not give up until he is forced to give up. When he is tossed into the Lake of Fire, it will be the end of his tyranny. Until then, he works to take as many people with him into that fire as he possibly can.

Over generations, one thing after another has been introduced into humanity's thinking. Meditation used for relaxation became meditation to reach a *higher consciousness*. This turned out to mean that the person's own inherent deity needed to come alive through self-actualization. Once this became firmly embedded and accepted as normal into the culture and thought processes, the next step is getting everyone on board for the coming *one world government*. Why is this important?

The one world government will be such that everyone will need to go along with it, or the government will take measures to remedy the situation. Anyone who balks at becoming a player in this government will be *set aside*, and that does *not* mean on the sidelines. It means people in droves will be executed. In order for this planet to achieve its own highest calling, the consciousness of all people must work together to bring this about, or they will die (cf. Revelation 6:9-11). Those who cannot join in will be eliminated.

People have been force fed the belief that *we can do it!* We can create our own reality! It is up to us to bring the changes needed to this planet and that can only occur when people set their minds to achieving that particular goal. Those who do not jump on that bandwagon will be "excused" from society altogether through imprisonment, execution, or both.

This is presented as if it is for the common good. People are being taught that the individual has no value. The world made up of *all* individuals has value. All must sacrifice for all. Individual needs and wants must be put aside because our very planet is at stake.

Whether they are *walk-ins, apples, fillers, soul exchangers* or something else along these lines, their goal is to *recreate* a person's thinking. Their job is to tune people into the "*higher frequencies*" of the brain's alpha waves so that we become susceptible to all types of teachings and suggestions from entities within the spiritual realm. Eventually, these beings will move in completely because they are *invited* to do so. From there, the goal becomes *total control*. Think of what it means to the world with millions upon millions of people throughout the globe having given their minds over to this type of *demonism*!

Once people begin to believe that the messages received while in the alpha state are *genuine*, it becomes very easy to open the door to these beings. In fact, once we *willingly* open the door to them, giving them permission to enter, they no longer need to encourage us to go into alpha state meditation. They can talk to us anytime because we were *willing* and they have accepted the invitation to enter.

Willing to Believe
People who are *willing* to open themselves up and listen to these entities, come to feel they are *safe*. They give themselves over because they convince themselves there is nothing about which they should be concerned. If there are any red flags, they push them aside as an-

tiquated remnants of ancient religious superstitions. They do not believe that these beings will do anything to harm them, though they have been given *no proof* at all of the beings' intentions. Because they *present* themselves as *loving*, *altruistic*, and *benevolent*, they are accepted as such by one human being after another.

Recently on TV, there have been a number of home security ads. The gist of it is that normally some friends are together in one of the person's homes. They are enjoying the time together because it is fun.

Eventually everyone leaves and the commercial makes it clear that one of the men who attended the party was not really *known* by the others, but he was *accepted* because he was good looking, friendly, and outgoing. He put everyone at *ease*. In fact, in one of the ads, a young man has obviously caught the fancy of the woman whose home hosted the party.

The woman says good-bye to her friends (including her new male friend who offers a warm smile in return), and goes back into her home, smiling at what a great time she had. She was probably thinking about that young man. Would she see him again? Turns out it would be sooner than later.

She just finished locking doors and windows and activated her home alarm system. At that moment, we see the same young man who was personable and affable, now at the back door. This time, he looks mean, bent on mischief and mayhem. The woman looks up, notices him, and is very confused, yet not alarmed.

The man breaks the glass on her door with his elbow and then kicks the door open. The woman screams, the alarm goes off, the telephone rings and instantly there is someone from the security company asking if she is all right. By this time, the man has fled, and she relays what has happened. The person at the security company indicates he is sending help right away.

What went wrong? No one at the party was able to *see through* this young man's *veneer*. He pretended to be something he was *not* and no one guessed. While in her home, he was simply playing along, casing the place. What was his intent? Was it robbery, rape, murder, or all three? No one would have guessed that this outwardly likeable young man was actually a cold-hearted thief or worse. Yet he was that, in spite of the fact that he pretended to be something else.

This type of misjudgment happens all the time in our society. Stars and celebrities are constantly mistaken for the people they portray on the screen. Even though some people believe themselves to be good judges of character, people can be very deceptive.

Consider a person overtaken by a being or entity from another spiritual realm. If human beings can deceive *other* human beings, how easy is it for these far superior spiritual entities to deceive *us*? It is extremely easy, especially when the only proof needed are *feelings*.

Suicide
How many times have you read or heard about some con artist who took someone for all the money he or she had? The victims describe the con artist as a very honest looking person, who was very likeable. No red flags went up at all. This con artist simply swooped in, *disarmed* the victim emotionally, and then when the con artist believed that the victim had gotten to the point of full trust, brought the hammer down and then fled, moving onto their next victim with the previous victim's money.

Most are aware of Megan's Law, which allows the average citizen to learn whether there are rapists, pedophiles, or the like in their neighborhood. Take the time to skim through some of the profiles and mug shots of many of the people on that list and one thing will be noticed. Many of these men look kind enough to cause no worry in anyone. They could be your next-door neighbor that you speak with daily. They do not necessarily send off any signals that make them stand out as a pedophile. In fact, many are extremely kind and friendly.

Some of the most violent criminals have been some of the nicest people! Ted Bundy comes to mind. I believe one of the reasons for that may be the fact that they are *possessed*. If not, then they are able to do what they do in the shadows (whether it is rape, murder, or both), and they learn to *separate* themselves as if they are *two* people. They can bide their time being nice to people because they know that eventually, their "dark" side will strike and relieve the pressure that becomes pent up within them. Knowing they will have that future release enables them to carry on as if they are nice, loving people because they will get what they want in the end.

How many times have you heard about the demeanor of people who end up committing suicide? Often, though not always, the individual has made the decision *ahead of time*, settling it in their minds, and because of that, in a weird way, they are at *peace*. The reason they want to kill themselves normally has to do with their inability to cope with life. They see no respite from the pressures they feel. They believe they have no other option and once they decide on that course of action, they come to terms with it and are *calm*. They realize that in a short time, they will not have to deal with those pressures any longer. They become *free*.

I personally know of three people during the course of my life who committed suicide. One was a young man in my son's junior high. His father came home and found him hanging in the garage by his neck. He had been dead for hours. During the few days prior to his suicide, people described him as carefree, fun, not bothered or stressed. This was different from his normal demeanor though, in which he always seemed under a great deal of stress.

Another individual was much older and earned his living as a sculptor – in his mid to late 30s – and the pressures of his life mounted up to a breaking point. He finally took his life, yet in the few days and hours before his suicide, no one would have guessed because he seemed to be at peace with the world! Of course, this is not always the way it happens, as many people kill themselves violently, or they are known to have been depressed up to the moment they ended their life.

To the demons that harass people enough to make them commit suicide, it does not matter. What matters is getting as many people as they can to leave this earth *without* salvation. They could care less *how* that happens, just so it *happens.*

To one person, they will teach them that suicide is the perfect out because they will leave their concerns and worries behind. To another, they will tell them that they are Jesus Christ or Michael, who has come to give them more insight that they will not find in the Bible.

Ultimately, this is what this whole thing is about! It is for **harvesting souls**. What may work for one may not work for another, so they try anything they can think of to keep people out of God's Kingdom. If it means lying to them about who they are, *fine*. If it means telling them what the person wants to *hear* about the next life, fine. It does not matter at all. Demons have no qualms about lying, because this is what they do. It is their natural language.

Chapter 3
Seth Spoke

JANE ROBERTS CHANNELS SETH

Seth, for those who are unaware, is the entity by which the person of Jane Roberts became known to the world. While there have been numerous individual strands of New Age thought, which have come together, multitudes connect Roberts either directly or indirectly with the actual start of the New Age movement in this country.

One Web site makes this claim, "*Seth is the internationally acclaimed spiritual teacher who spoke through the author Jane Roberts while she was in trance, and coined the phrase* **'You Create Your Own Reality.'**

Seth's empowering message literally launched the New Age movement."[18] Few would likely disagree with that declaration.

If we were to narrow down the thoughts, beliefs, and practices of the New Age movement, it could be summed up in this one statement by Seth himself; *each of us creates our own reality.* If we are miserable, it is because we ultimately want to be. If we are rich, or enjoy celebrity status, that is so because of our own creative efforts.

The story goes that prior to Jim Carrey's rocket ship ride to fame, he wrote himself a check for 20 million dollars and kept it in his pocket. He would spend time going to a high place that allowed him to view most of Hollywood and there he would meditate, using his energy to believe his wants into reality.

In time, Carrey did make it in the business and eventually, he actually received the sum of 20 million dollars for one of his films. He is famous, he is funny, and he is rich. However, is he *saved*? Carrey *seems* like a loving individual, speaking highly and emotionally of his father who passed some time ago. That sentimental reality though, colors his thinking and his attitude about life. Since he believes that it was through his own efforts that his 20 million dollar paycheck became a reality, why would he *ever* think that it came about not because of his own wishes and determination, but through the auspices of those entities within the spiritual realm?

"You Are God"

I have said this before, but it bears repeating. There is truly nothing new under the sun. Old things become new again through PR and updated packaging. The oldest lie ever uttered continues to be uttered today.

In the Garden of Eden, Satan bewitched Eve by informing her that God was really a *selfish* God. God did not care about Adam and Eve,

---

[18] http://www.sethlearningcenter.org/

because if He did, He would have told them *everything*. He certainly would not have placed limits on what they could eat in the very garden He had placed the couple.

Satan smoothly and without hesitation called God a liar, and then uttered *another* lie. This lie had to do with us, *humanity*. Eat of the forbidden fruit and you will be *like* God, encourages Satan to Eve. Your eyes will open to the truth and you will see for yourself what God is holding back from you.

Eve succumbed and so did Adam. The result of that was:

1. *Physical death began immediately*
2. *Spiritual death also came into existence*
3. *God cursed the earth*
4. *Satan gained control over this earth*

The lie that man can become a god, entered into the constant thought patterns of humanity with Adam and Eve, and it persists today. The deception that exists today is not that dissimilar from the lie that Satan originally said to Eve. In fact, he is *still* repeating it, and his minions follow suit, reiterating that lie as often as possible to snare seekers into a life riddled with disappointment, lack of fulfillment, and no relationship with God.

In 1963, Seth uttered to a gullible Jane Roberts, "*You create your own reality.*" It is fundamentally the same lie, but slightly *nuanced*. Unlike Eve and Adam, our eyes are already open to good and evil. Theirs were *not* and because of that, Satan had to tempt them with something that would make *opening* their eyes sound so attractive they would have an extremely difficult time resisting the temptation.

Therefore, the lie that was "*you will be like gods,*" is now "*you create and control your own destiny as your own god.*" In essence, it is the same lie because in order for us to *control* our destiny or *create* our own reality, we would of necessity *need* to be a god. This is a huge part of the loose-knit beliefs of the New Age movement.

The following is simply one excerpt of an audio of Seth's teachings, through Jane Roberts.

> *"Your beliefs form reality. Your individual beliefs and your joint beliefs. Now the intensity of a belief is extremely important...*
>
> *And, if you believe, in very simple terms, that people mean you well, and will treat you kindly, they will. And, if you believe that the world is against you, then so it will be in your experience. And, if you believe...IF YOU BELIEVE THAT YOU WILL BEGIN TO DETERIORATE AT 22, then so you shall.*
>
> *And, if you believe that you are poor, and always will be, then so your experience will so prove to you. Your beliefs meet you in the face when you look in the mirror. They form your image. You cannot escape your beliefs. They are, however, the method by which you create your experience.*
>
> *It is important that you here realize that you are not at the mercy of the unexplainable, that you are not at the mercy of events over which you have no control whether those events are psychological events or physical ones, in your terms.*
>
> *As I have told you, there is little difference if you believe that your present life is caused by incidents in your early infancy or by past lives over which equally you feel you have no control. Your events, your lives, your experiences,*

are caused by your present beliefs. Change the beliefs and your life changes." –Seth[19]

Our First Cause
In the belief system set forth by Seth, we become our own *first cause*. If your life is not a happy one, you have only yourself to *blame*. If it is a glorious one, you have only yourself to *credit*.

Granted, what we tell ourselves *does* have some impact on our thinking, our outlook, and therefore the quality of our lives even as Christians. The truth though is that this does not translate into being able to manipulate things so that we get what we want. In fact, it is the exact *opposite* of what Paul speaks of in Scripture, in which the Christian is to recognize God's sovereignty even in those situations, which are not palatable. In Philippians, Paul writes, "*I have learned, in whatsoever state I am, therewith to be content. I know both how to be abased, and I know how to abound: every where and in all things I am instructed both to be full and to be hungry, both to abound and to suffer need. I can do all things through Christ which strengtheneth me,*" (Philippians 4:11-13).

It is clear from the Philippians passage that Paul speaks of having learned the *true* meaning of contentedness. It is obviously *not* changing things to suit you. It is finding peace *within* each situation, whether the situation is initially pleasant or not.

We are taught in Scripture to praise God in all things (cf. 1 Thessalonians 5:18; Ephesians 5:20). We are *not* taught to seek to *change* things, nor are we taught to somehow learn to manipulate the physical universe to make a better life for ourselves.

By praising God in the midst of everything that comes our way, we are acknowledging His *Lordship* over our lives. By desiring to change things so that our life looks the way we want it to look, we are deny-

---

[19] http://www.sethlearningcenter.org/

ing His Lordship. There is nothing wrong in *asking* God to change circumstances. Even Jesus did this in the Garden of Gethsemane. He also prayed that only the Father's will would ultimately be accomplished, not His. That is our pattern we are to model in our own prayer lives.

This is *not* what Seth speaks of doing. He promotes a do-it-yourself mentality, based on a you-are-god falsehood. What of course is always fascinating with these demons who impersonate someone or something (alien, higher power, ascended master, etc.), is that they often mix truth with lies. It is routine, yet the uninitiated individual cannot distinguish between lies and truth because it all sounds so *inviting* and *captivating*. Since they do not view the Bible as authoritative, then they have only themselves to fall back on. They become their highest authority in determining truth from falsehood. As stated before, it is based on how they *feel* about something.

Here is an example of the lies *with* truth that Seth was so fond of spreading through Jane Roberts.

"(After death) you will find yourself in another form, an image that will appear physical to you to a large degree, as long as you do not try to manipulate within the physical system with it."[20]

At first glance, there does not really appear to be anything wrong with that statement. In fact, it tends to remind of Jesus and His post-resurrection body. He was physical, yet He was not physical, able to hold food in His hand, but also able to walk through walls. What Seth leaves out is that in order to have this type of body, one must receive Jesus Christ as Savior.

Here is another *Sethism* about the afterlife. *"The afterdeath environments... are generally far more intense and joyful than the reality you*

---

[20] http://www.sethlearningcenter.org/

now know."[21] Again, there is nothing generally wrong there. For authentic Christians, this sounds like a description of *heaven*. I have thought for the longest time that heaven will be "heavier," or "thicker," much more alive in many ways. This life, compared to it, is likely but a dream. Of course, Seth *innocently* leaves out the part about the fact that only those in heaven after this life will experience what he describes. Except for the fact that he uses the word "joyful," he could also be describing *hell* too, and its intensity.

Seth also spoke on scientific things like time. *"As I have said before, time as you think of it does not exist."*[22] That particular statement is fully true. Time was created for this earthly realm. Time does not exist in heaven. It may not have existed at all prior to the fall of Adam and Eve even on earth. Time and the Second Law of Thermodynamics work in tandem. As time goes by, things left alone, go from order to disorder, (except of course where evolution is concerned, which somehow circumvents this law...*uh...sure*).

On the concept of our own inner deity, Seth stated, *"Do yourselves just honor, and in doing yourselves that honor, you will see within yourself, the 'gods-in-becoming' that you are."*[23] This particular lie is probably one closest to Satan's original in Eden. Seth further indoctrinates all with the following words: *"I am trying to tell you that if you look inward, and study your own sacredness and creativity and blessedness, and joy and power, as closely as you study the sacred books of the gods, then you would realize that all those books of the gods were based upon the great reality of the individual, the individual soul, and therefore based upon your own reality."*[24] Again, the emphasis here is on each person's *inner* deity. Think about something though. Does anyone actually talk like this? Because the speaker is some entity from

---

[21] http://www.sethlearningcenter.org/q_after_death.html
[22] http://www.sethlearningcenter.org/
[23] Ibid
[24] Ibid

another world or dimension, it is given an audience. It sounds intellectual. It sounds as though it knows what makes us tick. In reality, all it is doing is catering to the ego found within each person. Ego will take every compliment it hears, puffing itself up, under the guise of having received *truth*.

Again though, *where is the proof* that any of what Seth states is true and accurate? Seth talks a good game, telling people what they want to hear (itching ears anyone?). He offers absolutely nothing that verifies what he says and no one *ever* asks him to do so. His words are simply taken *as* truth without question.

Seth's Christ
Of course, Seth does not leave Christ out of the picture completely. As in most New Age circles, Christ is *not* Jesus Christ of the Bible per se. Christ is best understood in terms of a *consciousness* that resides within *all* human beings. *"But behind and within those [religious] myths are the realities of your being - the Christ and the Buddha are both within you, for they are symbols of what you are. Pray to them and you pray to the hidden gods within you. You do not need to kick them aside like a child irritated with his toys!"*[25] Here, Seth states that Christ and Buddha are on the same playing field. They are *equals* in the game of life, all part of the grand scheme, designed to bring every human being to their pre-appointed destiny, which is self-actualization of our inner deity, in order to be our own gods. Wow. Who would not want that?

There are at least eight books by Seth and by that, it is meant that Seth spoke through Jane Roberts while someone else dictated or took notes (usually her husband). The first book *Seth Speaks,* deals with such topics as *"what to expect after death, how to glimpse into past lives, ways to contact friends and relatives who have died, dreams and*

---

[25] http://www.sethlearningcenter.org/

out-of-body experiences, lost civilizations, and much more."[26] This remains a very popular book within New Age circles.

Of course, the tragedy is that while people argue about the Bible's integrity and veracity, multitudes have read these books and view them as absolute truth, without question. To these people, God is obviously *not* powerful enough to get *His* thoughts down on a scroll, to be passed down through the ages written by over 40 people, but apparently Seth and any number of channeled entities have no problem in that area.

It obviously has to do with the fact that people are hearing these words *now* in their lifetime, by some medium or channeler. There are plenty of videos online attesting to this. This is tragic because while honoring demonic entities that tell lies routinely, as part of their nature, God is dishonored and made to look like someone who is unable to control things to His liking. He must instead rely on the whims and fancy of human nature.

I looked over one Web site that sells books and allows customers to leave comments. In one instance, there were 103 comments left by people. Of those comments, 86 gave rave reviews of *Seth Speaks* and gave the book five out of five stars. Five individuals gave the book four stars, four people graded it with three stars, two with two stars, and a total of six gave the book one star.

It is obvious that intelligent and sincere individuals wrote most of the reviews. Their desire is to share their feelings and understanding about Seth, Jane, and the books with sincerity. Here is merely a sampling of what people believe about Seth and his teachings.

- *"This was the first Seth book I ever read. It radically changed my perception of the reality I see with my outside eyes because*

---

[26] http://www.sethlearningcenter.org/index.html#books

it helped me begin to understand and recognize the reality I had been seeing all along with my inside eyes."

- *"This is a book for spiritual seekers! I was introduced to this book nearly thirty years ago by a dear friend who recognized I was seeking enlightenment. This was the beginning of a spiritual journey for me that had become thwarted after I had become an agnostic.*
- *"Even though I have since returned to my Christian roots, I embrace the idea that all spiritual traditions that enhance the soul are equally valid. For this reason, I would recommend this book to anyone regardless of their religious beliefs. It is a book about embracing your spirit. It is a book about finding your way to spiritual truth."*
- *"Seth has been one of my greatest teachers and I hope that you enjoy his presence, which is actually palpable for many, myself included. I spent a year with Seth, and my life was different afterwards."*
- *"A journey into the inner world unlike no other. Seth, an entity who spoke through Jane Roberts, takes his readers on the wildest ride imaginable."*

What can be said? People are being radically deceived, yet believing that they now have the truth. Even many who say they are Christians are coming around to believe that all roads lead to God.

Chapter 4
Archangel Michael

There is no shortage of entities vying for humanity's attention. Archangel Michael is merely one of many. A number of people claim to channel messages from this Michael. In spite of the fact that Michael the Archangel of the Bible says very little (with the exception of Jude v. 9), he apparently has a lot to say to us humans outside of Scripture, but he has only chosen a few individuals to speak his messages through.

He is described in this way: *"Through many succeeding cycles of time, as Ray after Ray provided The Pathway for the descent of new Spirits, Lord Michael has remained as the Guardian Overlord of the Angelic*

Host, the Elemental Kingdom and humanity. He shall not fold his Cosmic Wings about him to return home until the final Angelic Being is freed, the last man is redeemed and the last Elemental returned to its perfect state. This is the love of Lord Michael, who like many others, is a Prisoner of Love to the life he serves.

"*Archangel Michael is referred to as the greatest of all angels in writings throughout the world, including Jewish, Christian and Islamic.*"[27]

Ronna Herman is one such individual who claims to be a channeler by which Archangel Michael speaks. The messages are interesting and sound very much like the verbiage used by some ancient people who have learned English as their second language. In this case, the language is learned perfectly without the slang and the "g"s are not dropped. If a human being spoke like this though, we would probably give him or her no attention at all, because they would sound arrogant. Yet, because an entity from another world or dimension speaks this way, we receive their kingly speech without question because it reminds us of days when lords and ladies walked the halls of great castles. Here is an example of one of his messages that was transmitted recently, during the month of May 2010.

"*Beloved masters, those of you who are the Star Seed, answered a resounding clarion call that reverberated throughout this universe. You came from far-distant star systems, galaxies and solar systems, and you brought with you a wealth of cosmic information which was stored within your Sacred Mind for future access. There were stringent requirements you had to pass and solemn vows you had to make. You agreed to come to Earth during these momentous evolutionary times and to incarnate into greatly diverse and often very difficult circumstances. You made a pledge that when the time came for you to step onto the path of ascension,* **you would allow us to set aside your free will so that we could take whatever measures were deemed ne-**

---

[27] http://www.ronnastar.com/starquest2.html#2

cessary to awaken you*. For many, it resulted in a Soul merge, and others who had already awakened to their Soul Self were ready for a merge with a facet of his/her Higher Self. When the Soul finally merges fully with the Sacred Heart, it is a grand reunion of monumental proportions. When your intentions are composed of wisdom overlaid with love and projected with purity, you become a powerful source of Sacred Fire energy.*"[28] (emphasis added)

Note the bolded text from the quote above. Does that not scare you? Michael says that because people invite them that invitation gives them carte blanche to do whatever they believe is necessary to "awaken" human beings. THAT should terrify because what it ultimately means is that they can have absolute and total control over the individual human being.

Sci-Fi Movie Anyone?

People take this type of message seriously, but in truth, this could be from a Sci-Fi movie script. Honestly, who talks like this? The Lord of the Rings movie trilogy is loved because of the characters and settings, but also because of the *chivalry*, both in word and deed. Most of us have a much-romanticized view of the days of knights, castles, and life during that time. We forget that they ate with their hands and death could come at any moment.

Nevertheless, because of the way these messages are presented to humanity, people believe it more easily. They do this because it sounds *royal*, as if in a king's court, and comes with an air of authority. This is certainly befitting because the message is that we are royal, we are gods. Read it again and this time, pretend the dialogue is being stated by an actor in a movie, or on a stage. Notice how often the entity used the word "sacred". Your mind is sacred, your heart is sacred, and the specific fire referenced is sacred, like something out of Shakespeare.

---

[28] http://www.ronnastar.com/latest.html

Another individual by the name of Carolyn Ann O'Riley has a Web site that also claims to channel this same Michael. In a message given to O'Riley by Michael also in the month of May 2010, this Michael stated, *"Greetings & Salutations My Beautiful Beings of Light. Your brilliant beaming beacons of light precede your personal energy fields reflecting stressful life styles and chaotic world events. My Beloveds, bravo for working your hardest to keep your light vibrations as high as you can during times of major stress on your human physical forms.*

The Creator beams you down a ray of Golden Light to wrap around your shoulders. Just sit with it for a while. The more you can transmute stress using this wonderful golden beam the less stress your physical body will have to endure. This is a wonderful etheric golden beam that can be placed upon an etheric spiritual coat hanger for safe keeping and reused as needed within your spiritual imagination to assist your body to dispel harmful stress hormones.

The Earth Mother is indeed moving, shaking, belching and oozing all types of materials trying to also manage her vibrations during such times as were foretold of changes to the Earth."[29] It appears as though this Michael uses different verbiage and a completely different style of speech when speaking to and through O'Riley. It seems to be short on chivalry and long on pragmatism.

This Michael has a completely different way of speaking. He seems more "up," and excited, not so heavy in archaic monarchial speech. Think Captain Kirk with his cadence and emphasis as he speaks. It becomes a bit comical when seen in this manner.

Maybe Michael's simply in a better mood, and not so somber when he speaks through Carolyn. Kind of reminds me of Errol Flynn from Robin Hood. *"What ho, m'lady! Where art thou from? Wouldst thou seek solace of yonder castle? Come, I bid thee, stay and sup with me!"*

---

[29] http://www.carolynannoriley.com/AMMessageUpUPAway.htm

Notice also, what Michael has stated about the Earth (last sentence of the quote). Earth has just about had it, and in order to move to the next evolutionary stage in its spiritual development, it is doing everything it can to cast off the old, in preparation for the new. This of course, would explain all the *earthquakes*, the *floods*, the cold temperatures and longer winters, as well as *tornadoes* all over the world. It could not be due to what Jesus described as the "beginning of sorrows" in the Olivet Discourse.

The remainder of Michael's message deals with learning to fly spiritually, through astral projection, or soul flight. It is incredible the lengths these fallen beings will go to perpetuate a lie in order to deceive. They are very good at what they do, and have successfully deceived millions into hell. Fellow authentic Christian, these people need Christ; the *real* Jesus Christ, not some unauthenticated faker who pretends to be something he is not.

Yet Another Michael
Still another individual claiming to be the channel for Archangel Michael is Rev. Daniel Neusom, of the Sacred Light Fellowship (who also claims to channel Archangel Raphael). There are many video messages on the Internet from Nuesom channeling some entity. It is interesting the way he speaks when channeling, the way his head moves slowly from side to side as he speaks like an automaton. This almost becomes hypnotic and because of this, the messages take a while to come out. There are many pauses between words and phrases. All this, with that mechanical side-to-side movement of his head, make for a unique presentation.

In one of these transmitted messages, Michael speaks to us saying, *"You deserve...to be fully free... and fulfilled...on the earth. You were created to be... fully free... and fulfilled...on the earth. It is god's will...that you be...fully free... and fulfilled...on the earth. I am Michael of god's...light...who speaks to you now...through the energy and consciousness...of this channel...of god's light. You are a channel of god's light...if you choose...to be. Being a channel of god's light...is very natural...to you."*[30] The entire message is just under thirty minutes in length and the quoted section above took about two and a half minutes to hear due to the aforementioned pauses. Neusom also over enunciates dramatically. It is as if Archangel Michael has a hard time speaking through Neusom and he has not quite got the hang of using the muscles of Neusom's mouth.

Now, if we stop and repeat the message above in a normal voice and with a normal cadence, the message has no real impact. Try it. Say it out loud and see what you hear. However, say it slowly, enunciating carefully, with many pauses and it becomes much more striking. Can you see people hanging on every word? Yet, what did Michael say? He said (repeatedly) that we were created to be *fully free*. That is true, but freedom does not come through self-actualization. It comes through submission to God and full dependence upon Him for His salvation. Michael conveniently left that part out of the equation.

When all is said and done, Archangel Michael is an entity who is *selling* the same hocus-pocus as all the other entities. However, some entities are more highly revered and respected. Please note also that in Carolyn O'Reily's transmitted message from Michael, that entity refers to humans as his *master*. This also goes along with Christian thought that human beings will rule over the angelic hosts (cf. Colossians 1:18). It also feeds the *egos* of those within the New Age, because they will come to believe that they are really something, if angels refer to them as master.

---

[30] http://www.youtube.com/watch?v=DVr2mgf-U2c

Chapter 5
Kryon, of the Magnetic Service

I magine someone coming to your door and ringing the bell or knocking. Not expecting anyone, you approach the door just a bit leery, kicking yourself for not having put up the "No Soliciting" sign quicker. You open the door and you see an individual. He looks human, but he has some features that are not human.

You then notice that he appears to be wearing a costume. This costume has no cape, even though you think that he is trying to portray a superhero. You are not sure whether you should laugh, or slam the door. You look at the individual and say, *"Yes? May I help you?"*

The individual looks at you and with all seriousness, places his closed fist over his heart and says, "*Greetings, dear ones, I am Kryon of the Magnetic Service.*" You wait for him to smirk or laugh because you believe that this must be a joke someone is playing on you. You look around to see if you can spot any candidly hidden cameras. Nope.

In a situation like the one described above, who among us would take that person seriously? Kryon, of the Magnetic Service? *Kryon.* (A brand name of paint comes to mind). *Magnetic* Service? What in tarnation? This is how Kryon addresses people during one of his transmissions.

Kryon and the U.N.
Out of all the entities and self-proclaimed deities that exist within the confines of the New Age, some entity comes along who has more to talk about than simply the subject of love. After all, that gets old quickly if you stop to think about it, except for those individuals who are so softhearted that they find it very appealing to embrace that emotional side of life on a moment-by-moment basis on the verge of tears almost always.

So out of the mix comes someone like Kryon. Kryon is described by some as God, separate from the earth plane, or from Mother Earth. Others describe Kryon as a higher intelligence, here to teach humanity the way of love *and* peace, not just love.

I have to say that this Kryon tends to go out on a limb when speaking of peace. By that I mean that he is willing to speak in more specifics than many of the other entities who simply speak of freedom, fulfillment, and love. Kryon has – through *Lee Carroll* – spoken to members of the *United Nations* in the past. In fact, since 1995, "*Kryon was invited to come to New York and channel for the Society of Enlighten-*

ment and Transformation) S.E.A.T, ... a member of the United Nations Staff Recreation Council."[31]

That is an interesting thing when you stop to consider it. Here is a man (Carroll), who claims to be the channel for Kryon to speak to humanity, who was invited to the UN, and essentially gave an audience.

I will not bore you with all the verbiage (it is incredible how some of these enlightened entities can ramble on and on! You would think higher intelligence would mean an *economy* of speech, but...nope). I did find a very interesting tidbit about the Middle East situation, which I thought I would share here. You can decide what you think about it.

Now remember, these demons *lie*. That is their native language; however, this does not mean that *everything* they say is a lie. It means that they easily mix truth *with* lies so that it becomes difficult if not impossible for the uninitiated to determine when they are lying and when they are telling the truth.

I have found that quite often, these demons actually relay *truth*, but they wrap it in a package of *lies*. I have discussed this in one of my previous books and it is fascinating to see how much truth they will mix with their lies. Deceived people have no problem at all swallowing everything that is said, hook, line, and sinker.

In 2009, when Kryon shared his wisdom with the folks at the UN, he spoke of the Middle East problem and what he believed might very well be the solution. Oh, that's another thing they do. They will also caution their listeners about taking their words and statements as absolute FACT. While they are speaking, they are imparting facts; however, the oneness is always on human beings. We make or break the deal and by presenting it this way, they are never seen as liars. If

---

[31] http://kryon.com/k_un.htm

it does not happen, oh well, it is because there were not enough humans who believed it or some such nonsense.

Anyway, check out part of Kryon's message in 2009 as he spoke through Lee Carroll:

"It brings me now to the prophecy I've been giving for some time. For it remains strong [the potentials have not changed]. One of the most unusual things that you ever, ever could imagine may happen, and it involves Iran. I will say it again to you as I've said three other times to three other groups. Now I will state it in these halls of the United Nations. Iran may hold the key to the most stable, most profitable, most influential nation in the Middle East. And if this potential is fulfilled, it will be the young people of Iran who will create 'The Great Iranian Revolution'."[32]

Are you starting to see something? Here is more:

"The last thing you're going to see or imagine you would ever see has a strong potential to happen. The potentials are that Iran will actually invest in the peace of Jerusalem and that their influences and their funding will begin to have great influence for a solution in Israel – not just a solution between Israel and those called the Palestinians, but a greater one that creates solutions with the Islamic states around them."[33]

Huh? What? Did Kryon just say that there is a great possibility that Iran itself will be the major promoter of peace in the Middle East? These statements were made back in November of 2009, which of course was not that long ago. Last November, Ahmadinejad was every bit the anti-Semite that he is now. Yet, Kryon is telling these people at the UN that over time, a new generation of Iranians will

---

[32] http://kryon.com/k_un.htm
[33] Ibid

rise up and approach the entire problem of the Middle East in a completely different manner.

Kryon has even more to tell us. *"You will see the countries around Iran join with Iran, even former enemies. Borders will be relaxed. Eventually, it will affect Pakistan and Afghanistan, who won't want to be left out of the new Middle Eastern union. India will also be involved in a way that embraces Pakistan in trade like never before. Those who feature old energy thinking will have no place to hide, for peace will be the way of it. A brand new idea will emerge that says, "If we can stop the traditions of hate now, and teach our children to hope, eventually there will a group of nations who will only remember what the tensions used to be, from reading their history books."*[34] It's an important generation that is coming, one that can think ahead, way past their own lives... past their parents' teaching of old hatred and old ways. This, indeed, is part of the new rift that will develop between parent and child for the next 50 years in the Middle East.

He also told the people listening *"This is what we see and it is within the lifetime of many here. It may go slower, depending on what you do. It may go faster, depending on what you do."*[35] No prophecy can be given by these entities *without* the general disclaimer at the end, which absolves them of any real responsibility. Almighty God – Everlasting Father – Jesus Christ, King of Kings – on the other hand has *specific* times and dates and none of His prophecies are dependent upon humanity at all. His will and purposes come to fruition at the EXACT moment He foreordained that they would.

Can we put stock in what Kryon tells us? No, we cannot. However, I believe that within all of these statements, there is some truth. These entities see the truth they can see and use it for their own agenda. The young woman in Acts who became the carnival barker for Paul

---

[34] http://kryon.com/k_un.htm
[35] Ibid

and his companions spoke the truth. What the demon said through the woman was absolutely true, *"These men are the servants of the most high God, which shew unto us the way of salvation."* (Acts 16:17b). The problem though, was that Paul did not like the idea that a servant of Satan was actually barking out that truth and rightly so.

False Impressions Based on Truth
Therefore, between this and numerous other statements in the New Testament, we know that demons *do* tell the truth. Sometimes, what they do NOT say makes them a liar, because of the false *impression* their words give.

So here is Kryon revealing what *he* says will come to pass in the Middle East. Ultimately, he states that the people in the Middle East will solve the problem of the Middle East! Interesting, isn't it?

Those listening had no clue that this may in fact, be the absolute truth. However, Kryon neglected to go into the many details related to that peace and the fact that any brokerage of peace in the Middle East will be handled and overseen by Antichrist. Why bother with the details?

What I actually find even more fascinating than anything Kryon said, is the fact that he has actually spoken to groups within the UN and not just once, but *seven* times! How does THAT happen? It happens in a world where people want to believe that they are their own god, and that the all-powerful, all-knowing God of the Bible does not really exist at all. *That* is how it happens.

In another message, Kryon expounds on the subject of DNA, but before he gets there, he opens like a pastor in a pulpit (from a bad Sci-Fi movie like *Plan Nine from Outer Space*). *"Greetings, dear ones, I am Kryon of Magnetic Service. This is a family gathering; at least, that is the way I see it. It's a precious gathering, for if you really truly understood what was happening in this moment, I think you would be sur-*

prised. However, it seems so linear. A man sits on a stage, the music plays, and Spirit comes forth... and there is reverence, blessed energy, and respect. That's the way you see it.

"What is really going on here is so much bigger, for this day there's an allotment, **a permission that you have given for this energy to visit you from the other side of the veil***. This doesn't happen without people in front of my partner. He cannot do this alone. He cannot speak out loud with the voice of Kryon unless you are here, and he never has. This should tell you that there are some attributes in the process that require a 'give and take'" and there are.*

"You see, from my perspective, the entourage comes in and waits for permission. It's not a man on a stage. It's not necessarily a presentation. It's a reunion. For in the chairs in front of me, and reading and hearing, are ones I have known for eternity. All of you are eternal in both directions. There is no beginning of you. Think of this! That should tell you the essence and the core of what is inside.

"In this moment, in these times, in this brief thing you call channelling, there is energy given. It is information in English, but while it is given and while the energy is there, the third language is above you all. It visits every chair and asks the question, 'Do you remember?'

"The Human Being is not built for total spiritual recall of who you are on the other side of the veil. **If we offered empirical proof that this channelling was true, there would be no test at all***. In addition, the crowd would be so much larger, you know?* **If there was proof, everyone would be here***. No, instead it requires individuals to go inside and ask for discernment. 'Could it be that all that is being presented here is accurate and true? Could it be that it's exactly what Kryon says it is?' This is the discernment we have spoken of often, which the Human Being has available.*

*"So in these moments, there is, indeed, energy flowing from this crack in the veil that **you have given permission to open**. From that crack pours the energy of home. Just for a moment, with this third language, just for a moment, let it fill your heart. And if you're paying attention, it ought to fill you up with truth that you're more than you think.*

"All around this planet there is an awakening going on. It doesn't make a big noise, for there are no advertising campaigns or television shows that announce it. Slow, it is. Since 1987, it has been growing, and you feel it. Humanity is more aware of this shift now than ever before. Many around you are starting to accept what you in this room have accepted. Oh, they may not believe what you believe, but they are seeing who you are. They see a peaceful Human Being sitting among those who are in turmoil. They see the way that you handle life and others around you, how that makes a difference. There's a prophet inside each of you and we want to talk about that tonight. It may not seem like we're going to talk about a prophet inside when I tell you the subject, but there is. The subject is again DNA.

"So we would like to explain some things, and continue the teaching of only a few weeks ago that we gave in the top part of Earth [northern hemisphere], which we now bring to the bottom [Australia]. But, of course, that's if you look at Earth in a linear, popular way. For who is to say what is up and down? Perhaps it's even left and right? [Kryon smile]."[36] (emphasis added)

If you failed to notice, Kryon seems to take forever to get to his main point. He is so busy passing out compliment after compliment along with a host of "attaboys" that he really says nothing different than the old "this world is going through an awakening." Beyond that, notice how he covers his own rear end by talking about "proof" that what he says is true. In essence, he says there *is no proof* because if there was,

---

[36] http://www.kryon.com/k_channel10_melbourne_1.html

everyone would be there! He also says that ultimately, the people in that room were using *faith* (he calls it *discernment*).

Lee and We and the Harmonic Convergence of '87
Notice also that Kryon refers to Lee Carroll (the human channeler) as "my partner." If you take the time to watch videos on the Internet of some of these channelings, they remind of a church service, complete with Carroll leading in "prayer" to Kryon.

Please do not fail to see that Kryon also uses the king's English by referring to himself as "we." That of course is interesting because it tends to mirror the Christian belief in the Triune God, first evidenced in Genesis when God said, "Let ***us*** make man in our own image."

Kryon speaks of a veil that is cracking, a veil that allows humanity to see beyond it to who they are in their unadulterated form. This has been happening slowly, since 1987. What happened in 1987? Nothing less than a Harmonic Convergence, which took place from August 16 to 17, 1987. A Harmonic Convergence is the alignment of the planets, which to astrologers has always had significant meaning and some even connect the one in 1987 to the Mayan calendar (though scientists and astronomers remain skeptical). Kryon refers to this event without naming it, verifying that this particular event got things rolling in the spiritual realm. He also verified the authenticity of Harmonic Convergence events in general, which gives New Agers more reason to place their hopes and beliefs in them.

Kryon's big message has to do with DNA. By the way, more and more entities are channeling information relative to DNA, but why? It is obviously important and Kryon reveals how and why.

"We have told you that the DNA in your body carries with it a tremendous amount of unseen information and energy. We speak of DNA as an entity, not as a chemical double helix. That is to say, 100 trillion loops of DNA all work together as one energy to be called 'your DNA'" This

group is unique. It has to be, for it is absolutely, 100 percent you. Because of the quantumness of DNA, it can contain a huge part of your spirituality. This will be defined in the publication that my partner is working on now [Kryon Book Twelve]. Not only does DNA contain the record of all that you have been on the planet, but your relationship to Gaia as well. It contains all that you have ever done and the spirituality of what you've learned in every lifetime. This information is literally imprinted within it."[37]

What Kryon seems to be saying is that all of our spiritual experiences that *all* of mankind has had is contained in our DNA. Once science figures out how to break it open, there will be a shift in knowledge like no other. Let's all look forward to that, shall we?

Kryon continues. *"Now listen to me: Over eons, no Human ever loses any spiritual revelations they have ever had. Do you understand? With intent, any Human can awaken to the point at which their DNA holds what they've learned over all lifetimes. You awaken the DNA itself with your intent and epiphany of God inside. All of the spiritual things that you have learned will come flying back and be yours again. How could they not? You opened the door originally and you own them. This has to be good news to the individual who wonders what it's going to be like if he comes back. Will he have to start over? Will he have to go through the things again that he's gone through this lifetime? The answer is no. It remains free choice, and many lifetimes might go by without any kind of spiritual quest, but in this shift, many are beginning to "remember" who they are and what they know."*[38]

Here, Kryon of the Magnetic Service explains without saying it that all humanity is *interconnected*. We all share the same links to one another and those links go back for lifetimes. How many times have you heard this from other human beings and their beliefs? I remem-

---

[37] http://www.kryon.com/k_channel10_melbourne_1.html
[38] Ibid

ber in an interview years ago, John Ritter believed that a golden thread ran from one human being to the next, to the next and so on. It is not an uncommon belief that all human beings are interconnected.

Kryon shares even more news with the "congregation" through Lee Carroll. *"There is more. Within the DNA are attributes of the piece of God that you are. The imprint of the Higher-Self is there. The angelic name that I call you is there. That name is not a name in linearity or one spoken in the air with vibration. Instead, it is a name that we sing in light. And when it is spoken, it vibrates with majesty. That's the truth! Feel it! The imprint of who you really are is in there. You carry with you pieces and parts of the lineage from another planet and other areas of the Universe. The energy of those who helped seed you with humanity's spiritual portion are there as well [Pleiadian]. Appropriate, it is. Beautiful, it is. Loving, it is. All of that is there within your DNA, and in order for it to be there, it has to be a quantum energy."*[39]

It all comes back to our *higher self*, our *inner deity*. I personally appreciate where Kryon starts speaking in *Yoda*. "*Beautiful, it is. Loving, it is.*" Since most know of George Lucas' proclivities and interest in the New Age, it is not difficult to see the connection between his movies and his beliefs.

Kryon is not finished yet, and in fact, is just getting warmed up. *"The new information is that DNA provides a "field" around you that is interdimensional. That field is your consciousness, not your brain. That which your brain does is in tandem with the DNA. Your brain dreams... or does it? The synapse is there to show it, and in your deepest REM sleep, out comes so many complex things. Those things are all in your DNA, supplied to your brain. So the DNA even supplies instructions and influence to your brain's dream activity for you. These things are diffi-*

---

[39] http://www.kryon.com/k_channel10_melbourne_1.html

cult to explain, since we are not speaking about linear things, but that which is quantum."[40]

DNA is important, but infinitely more important is our *consciousness*. "The biggest attribute that we wish to discuss is this - this interdimensional DNA field is knowing. That is to say, it is built to extend life. It knows who you are. It contains the blueprint of your sacredness, and is one of the largest tools you have for health, for joy, for opening the door. It is in the DNA field, not the brain. That's where it is. And in that truth, there is celebration. For it releases you from having to create what you think you need.

"Let me give it to you this way. If you're going to use that field as a tool, now that you know what it does, you're going to work with your cellular structure to manifest things. The normal Human experience is to gather knowledge on how. 'How do I communicate? What is the best thing to ask for? How do I specify it so the DNA will know what I'm asking? Do I have to be a certain way or be in a certain place? Do I follow many steps that will open the door'?"

"None of the above! If you could visit your cellular structure, your Akash, your sacred life lesson, don't you think it would know what was happening? It does, perhaps even more than you do! All you have to do is speak to that which is the quantum part of you and it knows what you need. So we are asking you to relax the linearity of the lists that you give to God. For suddenly, we're telling you there is a quantum energy that is the sacred you who knows what you need."[41]

Kryon is now leading up to proving his theories from the Bible itself. "Let me review something with you that's ancient, wise, and tells a profound story. In your own scriptures in the western world, there is a story of a master named Elijah. This was the only Human Being in history to select his time of ascension without death and have it recorded by

---
[40] http://www.kryon.com/k_channel10_melbourne_1.html
[41] Ibid

the one who would take his place. Therefore, you could see it within the writings of the one who witnessed it. I want to review it, for even all the way back then, there is proof of the field.

"They say Elijah stepped into an opening, asking Elisha to record what was going to happen. Now Elijah was a master with great wisdom and knowledge and he is today what you would call an ascended master, and Elisha loved him. In the linearity of humanism, there is an entire group of people who expect his return. I have some news for them. Get out of your linearity, for he's been back a long time! For the energy of the masters are part of the energy of the great shift that is upon you. They intermingle with the vibration of this planet. They're all back, and it's what you're feeling. In a quantum state, they're in your DNA. Don't you sense this? There is so much expectation around 3D things that were never meant to be 3D. So much information is given in metaphoric terms, so you might understand that perhaps prophesy itself could mean things outside of your linear reality.

"Elijah walked into the open with Elisha watching, but he did not die. Instead, he claimed his sacredness. Indeed he left, but not without some fireworks. For Elisha indicated that he turned into a chariot of fire, accompanied by three entities. In the best that he could see and describe in his linearity, Elisha described what it looked like and what it felt like. Now, take a look at this, for you will find that it was not necessarily angels from above who came and got Elijah. Instead, something happened on the ground and Elijah turned into light and he left."[42]

Rather than castigate the Bible, or create doubt, Kryon has merely *explained* Elijah's "rapture" or translation to the heavens in empirically spiritual terms. I don't know about you, but I get *annoyed* when these demons deign to put a new twist on God's truth. They have no right because by doing so, they make God out to be a liar, placing new meaning on His truth, His Word.

---

[42] http://www.kryon.com/k_channel10_melbourne_1.html

Kryon the Bible Teacher

Kryon says that Elijah was able to leave this earth because he *decided* to do that and he did it by using the field around his DNA to make that transition. Kryon lies to the people, and they believe it. Suddenly, their mind goes, *"Oh, wow, so THAT'S what that means!"* No, it is *not* what that means, but since they have a voice channeled through a man who sits in front of them on a stage, who *tells* them what the Bible actually means, why should they disregard it?

It is not unusual to speak with New Agers and hear them quote the Bible. They believe their particular interpretation of it is accurate and the orthodox Christian's view is not. They believe that authentic Christians have yet to be enlightened or self-actualized as *they* are, and once accomplished, we will come to understand the Bible as *they* do.

Ultimately, what Kryon speaks of is no different than what other entities speak of, yet Kryon is far more descriptive. He makes his interpretation of the Bible and DNA sound much more scientific than ethereal. The reality is palpable because of how much Kryon *seems* to know about how the human body works. Kryon is obviously a powerful demon, one who likely ranks above many others. This ties in neatly to what Paul's referenced when he spoke of the fact that our fight is not against flesh and blood, *"but against **principalities**, against **powers**, against the **rulers** of the darkness of this world, against **spiritual wickedness** in high places,"* (Ephesians 6:12; emphasis added).

As an aside, imagine trying to exorcise Kryon from Lee Carroll. Imagine the fight that the exorcist would be engaged in during the process. Of course, in order to exorcise Kryon from Carroll, he would need to *want* to be exorcised for the most part. If Carroll fought against the exorcist's attempts, the battle would be that much more complicated. It is difficult to imagine Kryon giving up without a huge fight. Demon possessed people and attempts to exorcise them are not for the squeamish or weak in faith.

We will undoubtedly hear much more from entities like Kryon and Archangel Michael, as well as others. In fact, it seems that as time progresses, we can expect channeling to become much more readily accepted, until it likely becomes a type of normative way of living, fully accepted by the masses. It will in essence become like another news source, from the other worlds and dimensions to our world.

I am not saying that we should stop what we are doing and start paying attention to the messages of these entities that channel their speeches through human beings. What I AM saying is that we should recognize the fact that these entities are DOING that, and with greater frequency. Moreover, there are more and more people tuning into their messages, wholeheartedly believing and embracing them.

This is where the world is heading and the difficulty is in keeping this out of the church. Many churches – via the Emergent Church – have been overtaken by this spiritual deceit in some form or another. Christians need to be vigilant and of course, not give heed to these seducing spirits. We must not only NOT be taken in by them, but we must do all that we can to help others understand that the messages they are hearing may have some truth, yet nonetheless need to be ignored. We must also teach that the source of those messages has absolutely no interest in *our* welfare, but only in their own agenda. They wish to deceive in order to overcome. We must warn, whether they listen or not.

Chapter 6
Their Reality

There was nothing fake about the demons that Jesus and Paul cast out of people!

Consider the fact that the earth seems to be in a state of violent flux. We have been experiencing earthquakes seemingly as never before, along with droughts, flooding, volcanoes, tsunamis, and tornadic activity.

As I write this, numerous volcano eruptions have just occurred in the country of Ecuador. *"Explosive eruptions shook two huge volcanoes in Central and South America on Friday, forcing thousands of people to flee their homes and disrupting air traffic as ash drifted over major ci-*

ties."[43] On top of this, crops are dying off before they are harvested and there seems to be no real reason for this. For the past how many years, we have been told that Global Warming is a major threat to our existence, but just recently, it was determined that this belief might be a stretch, to say the least. In fact, unprecedented snowfall this past winter has left some areas of the world completely enveloped and not knowing what to do.

Beginning of Sorrows
Jesus stated toward the end, *"For many shall come in my name, saying,* ***I am Christ****; and shall deceive many.* ***And ye shall hear of wars and rumours of wars****: see that ye be not troubled: for all these things must come to pass, but the end is not yet. For nation shall rise against nation, and kingdom against kingdom: and there shall be* ***famines, and pestilences, and earthquakes, in divers places****. All these are the beginning of sorrows,"* (Matthew 24:5-8; emphasis added).

Jesus' words strike a chord with our world today, at least that's my belief. There has certainly been an increase in claims of Messiahship from many. From Benjamin Creme's indirect claim that Raj Patel is the man the world has been waiting for to release us from our captivity and bring us to the next spiritual plane, to other individuals who also claim to be this last Maitreya, the world is hearing these claims from one end to the other. These false prophets are deceiving many. False messiahs are found within the New Age movement, in one form or another. Roughly 2,000 years ago, Jesus warned that toward the end, this would become what seems to be common place, with many vying for the title of *Maitreya*, or *Imam*, or *Mahdi*, the last wise man who will usher the world into an existence of unprecedented peace.

Behind these entities are *demons*, masquerading as divine entities, here to help bring our world to the next level. There are very strange things happening in the world today and have been for some time.

---

[43] http://news.bbc.co.uk/2/hi/world/latin_america/10189054.stm

False messiahs, wars, and rumors of wars, famines, pestilence, and earthquakes in various places are all having their run. Christ says these are the beginnings of sorrows. *Sorrows.* That describes it. The earth, the people, the Creation itself is in sorrow due to the curse that God placed on it thousands of years ago because of Adam's sin.

The curse was actually to our benefit because it likely introduced the Second Law of Thermodynamics, which means simply that things run down to their stopping point. People die, animals die, and plants die. The earth itself is dying and nothing can be done about it.

As noted, Kryon says he has the answer and it all has to do with the coming vibrational shift that is scheduled to take place on this planet. Don't ask Kryon to be specific about the date though, because he will simply throw it back on you. It depends on how quickly human beings on this planet come together as *one*, he would say.

The people who believe that a messiah will come to rectify wrongs are in for a huge surprise. There *will* be a messiah of sorts. He will be an individual who will take the reins to the whole earth promising to extricate it from its lowly and worn out position to a place of *newness*. Many will believe him, only to find out later that it is all a lie.

It would appear that every aspect of the world's society is seeking explanations. This includes the field of science. Science has always looked to empirical evidence to reveal truth, or confirm it. This only comes through *experimentation*, *research*, and *observation*. This past December in Norway, science tried an experiment to determine the validity of *inter-dimensions*. A high-energy beam was fired into the heavens from "*the United States High Frequency Active Auroral Research Program (HAARP) radar facility in Ramfjordmoen, Norway.*"[44] Even though it was done in Norway, the United States was involved in this experiment (hence the name of the facility). If you stop to

---

[44] http://open.salon.com/blog/norwonk/2010/01/12/norway_unleashed_hell_on_earth

consider it, what *possible* problem could a high-energy beam shot into the heavens cause? No one knew, but found out.

Whoops!

According to more than one reporting agency, the facility in Norway succeeded in *puncturing* the sky with a 2.3-megawatt short wave signal. That seems weird, doesn't it? How could anything *puncture* the sky, since it certainly appears as though the sky goes on forever? If it actually *did* go on forever, then it would obviously be impossible to puncture it, but it looks as though scientists at the radar facility in question *did* in fact, punch a hole in the atmosphere. Why? They were searching for inter-dimensional *beings* or inter-dimensional *life*.

The article in reference states, "*To how catastrophic for our Planet this massive thermal inversion has been Anthony Nunan, an assistant general manager for risk management at Mitsubishi Corporation in Tokyo, is reporting today that the entire Northern Hemisphere is in winter chaos, with the greatest danger from this unprecedented Global event being the destruction of billions of dollars worth of crops in a World already nearing the end of its ability to feed its self.*"[45]

The ramifications are mindboggling, considering the fact that scientists are so concerned about it. The article goes on to say "*So powerful has this thermal inversion become that reports from the United States are stating that their critical crops of strawberries, oranges, and other fruits and vegetables grown in their Southern States, are being destroyed by record cold temperatures. The US is further reporting record amounts of snowfall in what they are now warning may be their worst winter in 25 years.*"[46] This article is from January 10, 2010. You will recall that the big question of Global Warming was put to rest due to the unprecedented cold and snow during this past winter

---

[45] http://open.salon.com/blog/norwonk/2010/01/12/norway_unleashed_hell_on_earth
[46] Ibid

along with allegations that the whole thing was a farce. Did this short wave radio signal have anything to do with it? Well, whether it did or did not, it could *not* have been good.

For those who have not heard of this event, nor seen the photos and video, here is a good link that shows both; pictures and video: *http://www.dailymail.co.uk/news/worldnews/article-1234430/Mystery-spiral-blue-light-display-hovers-Norway.html*

What is fascinating is that science itself is interested in moving beyond our *known* dimension into *other* unknown dimensions. Their desire is to see what, if anything exists there. Do things appear as an *event horizon* in which the very rim of a black hole can be seen as light is sucked into it in these other dimensions?

The fact that some believe that punching a hole in the sky *may* provide answers is a bit scary to say the least. This considering the fact that they really had no clue as to any potential problems that might be caused by such an experiment.

Spiritual Entities in the Spiritual Realm
The Bible provides many examples of spiritual entities that exist in the spiritual realm. It is obvious from Scripture that this realm exists *alongside* ours. The difference of course, is that we as human beings are at a disadvantage because generally, we cannot see into that realm. It is clear that the beings that exist *there* can not only see into *ours*, but also can and do come into ours and manipulate objects here as well.

In the tenth chapter of the book of Daniel, we read of a vision given to Daniel by Gabriel. This chapter bears mentioning because of its direct connection with the spiritual realm. Here we read, *"Then said he unto me, Fear not, Daniel: for from the first day that thou didst set thine heart to understand, and to chasten thyself before thy God, thy words were heard, and I am come for thy words. But the prince of the kingdom of Persia withstood me one and twenty days: but, lo, Michael, one of the chief princes, came to help me; and I remained there with the kings of Persia,"* (Daniel 10:12-13).

Notice that Gabriel was held at bay by some guardian referred to as the prince of Persia. For twenty-one days, Gabriel was kept from moving *beyond* this prince of Persia to take the answer to Daniel's prayer to him! This tells us a few things worth knowing:

1. We must persist in prayer until we receive an answer
2. There are obviously beings in the spirit world who have greater power and ability than some of the angels who never fell
3. This also means that there are ranks of fallen angels, with various abilities and strength

Why Gabriel had to go to Daniel by way of the prince of Persia is not revealed to us. When Gabriel has revealed to Daniel all that he came to disclose, he says to Daniel, "*and now will I return to fight with the prince of Persia: and when I am gone forth, lo, the prince of Grecia shall come,*" (Daniel 10:20). Gabriel essentially knew that he had to go back to God's throne by virtually the same way he had come to Daniel. Why did he not take a different route? The Bible does not tell us. The truth remains though that he knew he was in for a fight.

As Gabriel attempted to get to Daniel with the answer to his prayer, it was only after Michael the Archangel came to his aid that Gabriel was free to go on his way and deliver the message that God provided for Daniel. Why the prince of Persia or the prince of Greece would keep Gabriel from getting *back* to the throne of God is not revealed to us either.

The Bible treats these spiritual entities as real. I have outlined in a previous book where I believe these demons came from and why they harass us.[47] There are numerous cases of Jesus dealing with

---

[47] See *Demons in Disguise* and *Nephilim Nightmare* for more information.

demonized people during His lifetime on earth. In Matthew 8:28-34, we are told, *"And when he was come to the other side into the country of the Gergesenes, there met him two possessed with devils, coming out of the tombs, exceeding fierce, so that no man might pass by that way.*

"And, behold, they cried out, saying, What have we to do with thee, Jesus, thou Son of God? art thou come hither to torment us before the time?

"And there was a good way off from them an herd of many swine feeding.

"So the devils besought him, saying, If thou cast us out, suffer us to go away into the herd of swine.

"And he said unto them, Go. And when they were come out, they went into the herd of swine: and, behold, the whole herd of swine ran violently down a steep place into the sea, and perished in the waters.

"And they that kept them fled, and went their ways into the city, and told every thing, and what was befallen to the possessed of the devils.

"And, behold, the whole city came out to meet Jesus: and when they saw him, they besought him that he would depart out of their coasts."

It is clear here, if we are to take the Bible at face value, that these entities were and are *real*. It is also clear that the demons knew their future fate *and* they knew with certainty that it *was* going to happen to them. Moreover, there is never any indication in the Old or New Testaments that aliens exist, or higher powers, or ascended masters. They are all fallen angels, demons. The plain fact of the matter is that only in modern times have some decided that what Ezekiel and other prophets saw were alien spaceships.

Ancient Astronauts?
People like Eric Von Däniken have authored books in which they in-

fer from the biblical record that what the men of old saw and had a difficult time describing like Ezekiel's wheel in the sky and other anomalies, were aliens. Von Däniken's most famous book, *The Chariots of the Gods* describes visits from ancient astronauts. From the biblical account itself, we know that what Ezekiel saw was God's *glory*. Either we accept *his* understanding of the event, or we toss the biblical view aside, replacing it with our own modern interpretation. By doing the latter, we reject the veracity of Scripture and it becomes open season on interpretative exegesis. By sticking with the former, we acknowledge that God is God and is sovereign over all things.

By seeing extraterrestrials or ancient astronauts in the biblical record, we are merely superimposing modern beliefs on top of Scripture with no logical grounds for doing so. This view also reduces the Bible to something far less than God's authoritative Word that reveals His truth. Instead, it becomes a book filled with old stories about ancient civilizations. The only real purpose of these stories then is to testify to the possibility of visitations by aliens. In that case, the overall meaning is to point to outer space and how people understood these visitors from space long ago from their vantage point and cultural reference. The rest of the Bible simply becomes *filler* around which the story itself is built.

Another biblical insight is gained by always looking to see how Jesus Himself saw the biblical record. There are numerous times in which He referred to events that many people do not believe occurred at all in today's day and age. Whether it was the destruction of Sodom and Gomorrah (cf. Luke 17), the event of the global flood of Noah's Ark (cf. Matthew 24), or the fact that Jesus says He saw Satan fall from heaven as lightning (cf. Luke 10:18), the fact remains, that He is testifying to the absolute truth of Scripture. Because He does so, we need to take that to heart.

Biblical Veracity
When people cast aspersions on the authenticity of the book of Da-

niel, or Isaiah, or some other book, do we need to spend time debating them over the issue? In many cases, Jesus quoted directly from these books and Deuteronomy seemed to be one He quoted from more than others. The fact that He quoted from them and never questioned their authenticity should be good enough for us. If His testimony is not good enough, then nothing will be good enough.

It is obvious that Jesus understood the powers of darkness led by the master deceiver, Satan. In Matthew 4, we read where the Holy Spirit led Jesus into the wilderness for the express purpose of being tempted. Satan is here referred to in the King James Version as *tempter, the devil,* and *Satan.* In other words, he is a real being, not an idea.

It is clear that Jesus was speaking to an authentic *being*, a being that clearly existed. This is a being with enormous power and ability. He also has control of the kingdoms of this earth and has the power to give them to whomever he wants. Moreover, Satan *knows* the Bible and he used passages in his attempts to cause Jesus to sin.

There is no indication from Scripture – especially in the New Testament – that Jesus viewed Satan as merely a consciousness, or some higher power, or impersonal force. He obviously viewed him as a real, tangible, intelligent *being*. Jesus *spoke* to Satan as He would speak to another person. Jesus also stated clearly that Satan was a liar *and* a murderer (cf. John 8:44), attributes assigned to *people*, not to ideas or concepts.

Apart from Jesus, we have already mentioned that Paul cast out a demon from the young woman who followed him around announcing that he spoke the truth of how to be saved. Paul spoke *to* the demon(s) rebuking them, and casting them out of the woman in the authority of Jesus Christ (cf. Acts 16).

Peter refers to Satan by what he does, and how he works. He says, *"Be sober, be vigilant; because your adversary the devil, as a roaring lion, walketh about, seeking whom he may devour,"* (1 Peter 5:8). Notice that Peter states that Satan (the devil) is *as a*, or *like a* roaring lion. That is how Satan *operates*, but nonetheless, he is a real being.

Throughout the New Testament and in places in the Old, we see Satan as a unique individual, a being with tremendous power and ability. His most unique feature is his ability to *deceive*. Paul tells us that Satan can literally transform himself into an angel of light (cf. 2 Corinthians 11:14). It is not by accident that either Satan, or those who work for him, often come in some form of light, or make frequent reference to it. This is his favorite disguise, pretending to be the exact opposite of what he is in actuality.

It is from within the scope of his deception that he creates havoc and destroys. We see this in everything discussed so far, whether from Seth, Archangel Michael, Archangel Raphael, Kryon or some other entity. Satan and his underlings choose deception as their greatest weapon and why not? Is it any wonder that human beings do the same thing as criminals? When someone can pull the wool over another person's eyes, they have deceived them. When they have successfully deceived them, they gain control *of* them.

There have been many examples of how deceptive crooks can be. I remember one particular case that happened to the Green Grocer himself, Joe Carcione. You may remember him from the way he pronounced the word "vegetable" or from his tips about produce.

He had hired a man to do his accounting. One day, believing that the accountant was a man he could trust, Joe learned that the man had embezzled over $100,000 and simply disappeared. Because of it, Carcione was deep in the hole and had no choice but to claim bankruptcy. Initially despondent, but due to his remarkable faith in God, he bounced back! Though he had lost his store, his warehouses, his trucks and his business, through his radio show and newspaper column, he continued and gained an ever-increasing audience.

This is rare though as most of these situations end very badly, with people becoming deeply despondent from which they do not return. Too many con artists are able to gain the trust of people because they know how people act and react. A warm smile might not initially win someone over, but a warm smile day after day, along with a consistently enthusiastic personality may do the trick.

Con artists can be whatever they need to be to make their con work. It is their job and they do it well.

Some of the best con artists in history are:

- Frank Abagnale, who during a space of five years cashed fake checks worth over 2.5 million dollars
- Charles Ponzi, well known for what became known as a "ponzi scheme." His schemes, while seemingly real, did bring in money, but by their own nature, collapsed in on themselves eventually. Ponzi stayed with it until just before the collapse and then took off to start another one somewhere else.
- Joseph Weil, a con man who died in 1975, is believed to have stolen over 8 million dollars. He specialized in selling phony investments and was a master of disguise.
- Victor Lustig, a man who is credited with selling the Eiffel Tower. One of his schemes involved selling a machine that could produce one hundred dollar bills. He cautioned that the machine could only produce a bill every six hours. Some people paid thousands for one of his machines. When they took it home, true to form, it spat out a one hundred dollar bill, and six hours later, another one. After that, the only things it spat out were blank pieces of paper. The two hundred dollar bills were real. By the time people realized they had been had, Lustig had been gone for at least six hours.

Con Artists are <u>Believable</u>
There were many others, but the main ingredient that all of these con men shared was their *believability*. No one doubted them long enough to question them. Since greed often forces people to see a lie as truth, giving into a con often happens.

Stop and consider the fact that a person would be willing to pay thousands of dollars for a machine that could print one hundred dollar bills. The individual, who would put down money for that, deserves to be conned. They believe that they will be able to make their own money without getting caught, never mind that it is illegal!

Beyond that, it never crossed their mind to wonder *why* con man Lustig *needed* or *wanted* to sell the machine! Why would he sell it if it printed one hundred dollar bills? He was set and he certainly did not need anyone else's money because he could print his own. Moreover, the more people know about his moneymaking machine, the greater the chance of Lustig getting caught. None of it adds up, yet to those individuals who give into their own greed and avarice, sensible thinking is not part of the transaction.

This is exactly how demons and Satan himself works. He tells people what they want to hear. He promises to give them the things they crave. Because these things are presented in such an *altruistic* way, Satan's promises are often adopted without questioning the source or the promises themselves.

Unearthly Powers
David Burnett published a book titled, *Unearthly Powers*. In it, he takes the reader all the way back to what he considers to the primal and folk religions of ancient days. Understanding the nature of these things, and their origins helps authentic believers today comprehend more how Satan works in the world.

The author opens his first chapter by relating to the reader a trip he took to Uganda. Upon arriving in one of the villages, he was told that he was just in time to view a ritual sacrifice that the villagers were going ahead with, in order to bring rain to their dry fields. The sacrifice involved killing a bull, which had to be black. The black bull was symbolic of the black clouds filled with rain, that were the hoped for conclusion. Once the bull was killed, the carcass was stripped and cut up and prayers were offered to the god, Akuj. After the prayers, the roasted meat was passed around to the villagers to eat.

To the surprise of the author, though the sky had been clear, at about 3:00pm, black clouds gathered and rain fell in buckets. Certainly, this age old ritual goes against all the laws of science, and because of that, there must be a scientific answer to the question of why the sky turned from clear to rain in such a short amount of time.

The answer connects to what the author terms, the *primal worldview*. In this view, there is little to no separation between the natural and the supernatural, as there is in western culture. *"First, in primal religions, the universe is not closed – the border between the 'natural' and the 'supernatural' is blurred. The natural and supernatural merge into each other, rocks and trees may have supernatural powers, and spirits take on human forms."*[48] This particular worldview allows for a wider belief in the supernatural since there is little space seen between the two areas.

The people who have this specific worldview *"assume that various phenomena may be controlled by means of signs and rituals."*[49] The immediate problem is that these people see little to no difference in the various powers they experience. They have no ability to grasp any real difference. To them, one god brings rain, while another brings the sun. Both gods are capable of becoming angry and venge-

---

[48] David Burnett *Unearthly Powers* (Nashville: Oliver Nelson, 1988, 1992), 19
[49] Ibid, 19

ful, which requires the need for sacrifice. While there may be one supreme being or god over all others, the lesser gods are often comprised of divinities, spirits, and ancestors.

Throughout the world, many societies exist where some form of ritual sacrifices are offered. Beyond this, often spirits are worshipped and appeased in order to gain their favor for the tribe or group.

Inside Juju

Within the continent of Africa, there is a religion known as *Juju*. It is a form of witchcraft, or in actuality, demon worship. There are many rituals within this particular religion. However, within this religion is hidden another religion that is only revealed and known to those within Juju who are advanced in understanding and training.

This inner religion or advanced level includes gruesome and bloody rituals, and sometimes with humans as the sacrifice. This is because the gods worshiped in the Juju religion are gods to *fear* and must be appeased, unlike the God of Christianity. The only people who need to fear the Christian God are those who die in their sins, *without* salvation. In Juju, all gods are feared and must be appeased through rituals. The rituals that satisfy these fearsome gods are ones that spill a good deal of blood. The unfortunate part of this inner religion is that many of these rituals include the killing (sacrifice) of human beings.

Juju has made its way into America and is practiced here complete with ritual killings of animals. Juju in essence is *"the religion that is believed to give power through blood."*[50] We have all heard the stories of those who worship Satan and eventually find themselves performing some ritual killing *for him*, or *in his name*. Often, if these things are mentioned in the media, they are normally downplayed. We are

---

[50] Isaiah Oke *Blood Secrets* (Buffalo: Prometheus Books, 1989), 20

told that the culprits are simply kids, wannabe Satan worshipers. We are told that it is no big deal.

Law enforcement will also often downplay these events, primarily because they do not wish to set off a panic among citizens. The truth of the matter though is that these rituals exist. They are performed by people who firmly believe that through them, they will gain *power*.

Satan's Simple Goals

All of this plays well into Satan's goals and ambitions. Ever since he fell, when sin was found in him, his goal has been to rise *above* God's throne. He has always wanted worship and everything about the New Age, pagan religions, and many of the rituals that exist within them are designed for this purpose.

For the people he knows will never be part of any type of ritual killing he offers the New Age where *self* is worshiped and idolized. Once people come to believe that they are their own god (able to create their own reality), he has succeeded in causing people to deny the God of the Bible. If they deny the God of the Bible, then they are guilty of committing the same sin as Satan by default. Satan became so enamored with his own beauty and intelligence that he thought all worship should be directed to *him*, not God. This continues to be his goal today, and it is all working toward the day when the "man of sin," also known as the Antichrist, will take the stage as the final world ruler who will ultimately demand homage. Those who worship him will in fact, be worshiping Satan.

In this life, there are only two options when it comes to what or who to worship:

1. *God of the Bible*
2. *Anything else*

All people *will* bend the knee in worship to Jesus Christ, whether they like it or not (cf. Philippians 2:10), even those who have resolutely refused to do so in this life. Those who prefer to ignore God, wind up worshiping Satan, either indirectly or directly. The reason for this is because Satan has set himself up against the one, true God. If he can cause people to chase after things like money, jobs, homes, a trophy wife or husband, or go down the path of New Age mysticism, or even outright worship of other gods, Satan has succeeded in drawing people away from the God of the Bible.

Even atheists, agnostics, and skeptics are not exempt. Because they become their highest authority, they ultimately choose to worship intellect or reason. Is it any wonder the Bible tells us that the fool has said 'There is NO God!" (Psalm 53:1; also Romans 1).

Though Satan has masterfully created divisions, religions, and a variety of thought processes related to the concept of God, they are all essentially the same in the way they work themselves out in this life. There is little difference except for the outward rituals themselves. In the final analysis, everyone involved in anything other than Christianity ends up worshiping something other than God. In this way, all are guilty of idolatry, which is in the final analysis, nothing more than the worship of Satan.

In the Old Testament, worship of Molech involved the sacrifice of children. Leviticus 18:21 (and elsewhere) makes this perfectly clear when it states, "*And thou shalt not let any of thy seed pass through the fire to Molech, neither shalt thou profane the name of thy God: I am the LORD.*" The ritual normally involved placing the child on the arms of the large statue of Molech. Below his arms was a pit in which a bond fire was created. While a group of musicians played *in front of the* fire pit, the child was dropped into the burning pit, as Molech's arms would lean down (mechanically). The musicians were used to cover the screams of the child that was burning alive.

Ritual sacrifices like this were done to appease the gods, and that god is Satan. We might be tempted to think, "*Yeah, but then why did God ask Abraham to sacrifice Isaac if this was anathema to God?"* God answered that question by *stopping* Abraham before he killed Isaac and by telling him that He (God) knew that Abraham would not hold anything back from God. This revelation was more for Abraham's benefit, not God's since God knew already that Abraham would never withhold anything from God. Abraham would always remember that he was faithful to God in all ways (cf. Genesis 22).

God never allowed Abraham to follow through with the sacrifice of Isaac. By the way, no one during Abraham's time would have thought Abraham was doing anything out of the ordinary, since it was done so often. This is not the case today and God would *never* ask or expect any of His children to do something like that.

All rituals to Molech, Baal, or some other god always ended with some manner of blood sacrifice and/or death. These sacrifices were not done as a sin offering, nor were they done to point to Jesus Christ, like the Old Testament Mosaic sacrificial system. They were done for a number of other reasons:

1. *To counterfeit a type of sin offering*
2. *To teach humans to live in fear of a god's wrath*
3. *To kill human beings who would die without salvation*
4. *To be an acceptable worship to Satan*
5. *Blood carries the life of the body*

In the religion of Juju, there are many *required* ritual killings. These killings are done to conciliate their gods. As an example, in his book Isaiah Oke speaks of the fence around a small village or city in which Juju (or Yoruba) is practiced. The fence would have seven gates and the orisha (or spirit) *"in charge of gates is Legba. Legba is not a friend of man; no orisha ever is. But he is the enemy of Fate. And it is Fate that sends bad fortune to men. So we propitiate Legba in order that he will trick his enemy Fate into leaving us alone."*[51] The way Legba is satisfied is by taking three random individuals and burying them alive *"still kicking and screaming, under each of the seven gates."*[52]

In other situations, people are taken to the *Shrine*, which is part of the hidden or inner Juju. In one particular case, a woman in the tribe had been cursed to die. Death would come slowly only after being eaten by sores and flies. They took the woman to the Shrine because of the seriousness of the situation.

Once there, they began invoking the spirits and soon, the woman was writhing not in agony, but in *sexual ecstasy*. It was later learned that the spirit *Esu*, had possessed the woman and did what was called *spirit rape*. Esu as it turns out, is the equivalent of Satan in Christendom. We know from Revelation 20:10 that Satan's future fate lies in his occupation of the Lake of Fire. This will be his final and permanent home, from which he will never escape, nor will he ever be able to bother, harass, devour, tempt, rape, or cause to sin anyone again.

---

[51] Isaiah Oke *Blood Secrets* (Buffalo: Prometheus Books, 1989), 29
[52] Ibid, 29

Chapter 7

Their Purpose

As we have seen, *something* exists in a dimension that connects to ours, allowing these entities to enter and exit at will, something we are not able to do in our human form. We know that Jesus understood these beings to be real, not some figment of His or anyone else's imagination. We also know that apart from elect angels, these beings are up to no good. They have no desire except that which pleases their master, Satan. His desire is the full and total corruption of all of humanity as well as to be worshipped as God.

Loving to Hate

To these demons, human beings are to be hated, and they hate without effort. In their hatred, they have created a myriad of avenues and paths that appear at first to be good, in purpose. Yet, it is clear that no real good comes from any of it. Their messages, as they are filtered through human partners, are so littered with lies that it is often difficult to determine where the lie stops and truth might start.

So evil and determined are they to capture the hearts of human beings that they will seemingly stop at nothing to ensure the imprisonment of one person after another. When I stop to consider the many individuals like Jane Roberts, Ruth Montgomery, and others who have literally given themselves over to something they believed to be completely altruistic, yet was not, my heart grieves.

Messengers of Hope?

One after another, people are being caught up in this web of deceit promulgated by the powers of darkness, masquerading as beings of light. In one book, authored by Carol W. Parrish-Harra called, *Messengers of Hope*, Parrish-Harra outlines the mysticism to which many are called. Parrish-Harra herself founded and pastors Light of Christ Community Church, and considers herself a mystic, as well as a minister, author, and lecturer. Parrish-Harra has also been specifically identified by Ruth Montgomery as a *walk-in*.

Parrish-Harra believes the process of learning that a person is actually a *walk-in*, begins with an awakening to that fact. As to her own awareness of it she says, "*I now know it was the time when the original Carol 'died' and a new Carol arrived to begin her special task. The in between years of awakening to the new personality were lonely, confusing and frightening.*"[53]

---

[53] Carol W. Parrish-Harra *Messengers of Hope* (New Age Press, 1983), xiii

This realization came through a process known as *awakening*, which is essentially recognizing the fact that God exists and *"to the knowledge that we are more than our bodies, emotions or mind. Ultimately, as expansion of consciousness occurs, we integrate these aspects into a wholeness, a harmonious, smoothly operating personality into which spiritual inspiration can also flow. With this story of mine I will suggest to you another dimension, another connotation to "waking up."*[54]

Parrish-Harra wastes no time in connecting the alleged dots between ancient religious teachings the Christian Bible, in which Hebrews 13:2 tells us that we should treat strangers well, since they may in fact be angels. She then references the Hierarchy (aka Elder Brothers), *"of humanity who guide the earth both from the spiritual levels and from communication with adepts living on the earth. The adepts are those awakened beings who have mastered the process of integrating the personality to provide vehicles through which spirit may flow undistorted. These teachings speak of the externalization of the Hierarchy. This means that from time to time, when humanity's needs are great, some of the elder brothers (adepts),* **come into physical bodies in order to be of special service to mankind**.*"*[55] (emphasis added)

Parrish-Harra prefers to use the term *messengers* as opposed to *walk-ins "because it recognizes the reason for such an exchange in a more meaningful way."*[56] Her book unfolds with more of the Gaia, (or Mother Earth) New Age jargon, and experience. A poem she includes begins *"God, my Mother and my Father..."*[57] Throughout her book, the topic of love is the overriding concern, but it is not biblical love.

What I find intriguing, not just in Parrish-Harra's book, but the overarching issue with the entire area of the New Age, is how quickly a quantum leap in awareness and knowledge has seemingly already

---

[54] Carol W. Parrish-Harra *Messengers of Hope* (New Age Press, 1983), xiii
[55] Ibid, xiv
[56] Ibid, xv
[57] Ibid (no page number)

overtaken this planet. This is a fact that cannot be ignored. It is not merely this author's observation, but also many from within the New Age itself attest to the reality that even they are amazed (in a delighted way) that these giant leaps have occurred. It almost appears as though the earth itself is in a hurry to get somewhere.

The reality though is that what we are seeing is an ever-increasing form of *apostasy*. With this apostasy comes a greater spiritual influence on society and that spiritual influence does *not* come from God.

Think back to the times when the witch trials were held, or go even further back with the Roman Catholic inquisitions, when just about everyone was found guilty of something. Anything supernatural was considered taboo, and even illegal, worthy of torture, death, or both.

As time has marched onward, society has become much more comfortable with the idea of the supernatural and the spirit world. Unfortunately, many of these people continue to look askance at the veracity of the Bible believing it to be nothing more than volumes of stories that originated in *myths*. This is due in large part to the fact that the Bible is *old* and it was penned by humans. Because of this, and alleged contradictions (none of which I can find), the Bible is set aside as authoritative, and merely viewed as something from which we learn about ancient cultures.

Today is another situation altogether. People are much more open to the spirit world, the belief in reincarnation; the idea that deity resides within each person and we already possess all that is required is to discover it. Once discovered, it is then that the journey of the soul truly begins, whereas before, the individual was simply spinning his or her wheels.

Many people like Parrish-Harra are intelligent, sincere, pragmatic, and even altruistic, but also deceived. They firmly believe that what they experience is true, and that those experiences are designed to bring them to a higher level of consciousness, one in which they will learn how to create reality as they wish it to be. No longer will they have to settle for a mundane existence when they can instead capture *from* life whatever it is they wish to capture.

Remarkably, many of these people are also *happy*. I deliberately use the term *happy* as opposed to filled with joy because happiness can be fleeting and largely based on externals, whereas joy is often part of the redeemed soul and stems from within the person.

Parrish-Harra and others like her believe that when this experience takes place within, they have truly been awakened. *"I was to awaken from the anesthetic to a life more different than I could have ever dreamed."*[58] Parrish-Harra is of course, not the only one who sees it this way. Because she was awakened to the belief that she is a walk-in herself, she now sees life differently than the rest of us.

Parrish-Harra provides a reiteration of definitions based on Ruth Montgomery's work, *Strangers Among Us*. In this regard, there are beings that have access to the person and their body. Because of the numerous reincarnations allegedly experienced, *enlightened beings* can simply bypass the birth process and childhood itself. This allows them to enter into another body as an *adult*.

A walk-in is a spirit that is allowed to move into the body of a human being when the previous spirit wishes to leave. It is important to note that these walk-ins may only enter when *invited*. Even Montgomery makes a distinction between good and evil spirits, referring to specific cases such as *The Three Faces of Eve*, or *The Exorcist*. Because the latter are *obviously* evil, then they *are* seen as evil. Because other spirits seem to do *good*, they are seen as good (like walk-ins, enlightened beings, etc.).

---

[58] Carol W. Parrish-Harra *Messengers of Hope* (New Age Press, 1983), 1

The Bible's Record

The Bible makes no such distinction and in fact, never shows a "good" spirit possessing or trading places with a human being. The biblical record is clear that the only spirit that ever enters into a human being are evil spirits. Of course, it might be argued that there is no *known* example in the Bible of a "good" spirit possessing a human being, so we do not know. In this case, it might be argued that there could very well be examples that we cannot pinpoint. Unfortunately, this is nothing more than an argument from *silence*, which is not an argument at all.

According to Montgomery (and therefore Parrish-Harra, since she quotes her), the reason that walk-ins enter into a person's body is strictly for *compassionate* purposes. They only seek to help us, not harm us. They want us to improve, not destroy ourselves.

It is also clear that these walk-ins enter into a person's body with the original equipment there, so to speak, relative to the person's emotions, intellect, and memory (to some degree). Over time, the walk-in begins to blend (or is it usurp?) their own personality with the person's whose body they have entered. This takes time. *"He/she must now use this already developed form and seek to impress its personality with new vitality and ultimately exchange the old personality patterns with its own. This alteration is done slowly and is partially responsible for the trauma experienced by the incoming one. During this transition time, imagine the puzzling 'difference' that is felt at times by those around this changing personality!"*[59] Admittedly, those around the person *will* see a difference in personality and might possibly be alarmed.

Parrish-Harra states that, *"Probably there is no better time for such a change to occur than during what today is called the Near Death Experience, generally as a result of a serious illness or accident. It was in*

---

[59] Carol W. Parrish-Harra *Messengers of Hope* (New Age Press, 1983), 2

this manner that Carol, the original builder and creator of the physical, emotional and mental form, could depart and donate the vehicle to an incoming soul."[60] Repeatedly, the event that causes a walk-in to change places with the original soul is described as happening during a very traumatic event. As just seen, Parrish-Harra believes her soul exchange took place during her own Near Death Experience. This is a common belief. She goes on to describe the situation that caused the exchange. For her, the situation involved a being of light, who she calls the "Light Being." She also explains that she knew what was happening to her to be *true*. The thoughts she had, the experiences she experienced and the entire situation itself was true, because she "*knew them to be Truth.*"[61] That knowledge though, came directly from her feelings, her emotions. That was her proof.

Unfortunately for Parrish-Harra and millions of others, what she does not seem to realize is that truth has become subjective and relative. Her only means of knowing whether something is true or not is how she *feels* about it. Because of this experience, Parrish-Harra describes a new serenity that enveloped her, something she had never felt or experienced before. "*As this occurred, an intensity of feeling rushed through me, as if the light that surrounded that Being was bathing me, penetrating every part of me. As I absorbed the energy, I sensed what I can only describe as bliss. That is such a little word, but the feeling was dynamic, rolling, magnificent, expanding, ecstatic...BLISS. It whirled about me and entered my chest, flowing through me. I was immersed in love and awareness for an ineffable time.*

"*In the bright light of the Presence, courage welled up in me and the wonder of life and the secrets of the universe filled me as revelations which I was to recall at a proper time in the future. I felt buoyant and strong, prepared to let life lift and guide me.*

---

[60] Carol W. Parrish-Harra *Messengers of Hope* (New Age Press, 1983), 2
[61] Ibid, 4

"An intense rush of energy penetrated every part of my being. As I absorbed the pulsating love, bliss became my nature. I was whirled downward...outward. The feelings were dynamic, rolling, magnificent, expanding. Time rushed about in great swirls. There was no place to catch hold...suddenly, darkness. The heaviness of the physical body made itself felt. I let myself rest in that darkness, the tender, caring darkness of a womb. I was enfolded in the memory of great love."[62]

Parrish-Harra then goes on to explain her *new birth* by which she gained new insight, greater understanding, and a clarity she had never known prior. All of this happened when she gave birth to her own child in which she nearly died. She remembers seeing a *"Being with a magnificent presence. I could not see an exact form, rather a radiation of light that lit the heavens and it spoke with a voice that held the deepest tenderness one could ever imagine. The voice said, 'Look.' I looked into an area that suddenly was enclosed with a large golden frame. As I watched, a bright falling star moved from the upper corner and continued slowly, gently, across the framed space. As it got the lower corner, its light went out. The voice said, 'My child, do not be disturbed. Death makes no difference in the pattern. If you are, you always will be."*[63]

There are a number of troubling problems with Parrish-Harra's explanation. I do not doubt *her* at all or her *experience*. I doubt the *source*. Time and time again, you will hear teachers within the New Age say that God is in all and through all. They teach that we are all part of God. We are gods. Yet, I always find it fascinating when reading these accounts of these individuals who do not necessarily believe in one particular, personal God, they wind up meeting one particular being who they always describe as light and love. If we are all part of the same deity, then why does there need to be *one* being that represents God to them?

---

[62] Carol W. Parrish-Harra *Messengers of Hope* (New Age Press, 1983), 4-5
[63] Ibid, 3

What Do *Emotions* Teach?

The other difficulty is that we have to ask ourselves what it was that Parrish-Harra actually learned. Feelings of ecstasy overwhelmed her. She felt bathed in love and light, which she says permeated her entire being. She also indicated that she came to understand truths so vast and powerful, that words cannot be used to explain them. She came to conclude, *"consciousness is life. Human beings will live in and through much and this living consciousness, which we know is behind our personality, will continue. I knew now that the purpose of life does not depend on an individual; it has its own purpose."*[64]

Later on, she confesses that everything is different within her and that she knows so much more than she used to prior to her Near Death Experience. However, what does she actually *know*? It all seems to be rolled up in beauty, love and understanding. She eventually came to be *detached* from all that she had previously held dear, including her parents and even her husband. How is it that beauty, love and understanding helped her here? It actually drove her *from* the ones who loved her.

What I also find troubling is that following this Near Death Experience, Parrish-Harra's life was essentially *miserable*, to the point that she wished to die. How could the reality of love and beauty cause her to wish to die? Over the years following her Near Death Experience, she relates many situations that caused her to grow, some causing alarm, others creating serenity; all of them based on *feeling*.

When it all boils down to it, what Parrish-Harra learned is to rely on her *feelings*. It was through her feelings that she became aware of the fact that she was exchanging places with a walk-in, who took over where the original Parrish-Harra left off. It was through feelings and emotions that she would learn what love is, and she would learn that

---

[64] Carol W. Parrish-Harra *Messengers of Hope* (New Age Press, 1983), 4

there were no absolutes of right and wrong.[65] Those moral absolutes must go.

Poor Imitation of Christianity
In essence, what took place within Parrish-Harra is the exact opposite of what takes place within the authentic Christian. The authentic Christian moves *away* from a culture that teaches all truth is relative, toward God who is Truth. God has given us absolutes and these absolutes must be obeyed, if only because God has said they must. We can be certain that in learning God's absolutes and following them, we gain a greater *awareness* (not feeling), of the fact that God is love, yet that love has divine limitations.

With everyone in the New Age who claims to have *experienced* God, it always appears to be the same. Love (as *they* define it, not as *God* defines it), is the highest thing that matters. Love is a *feeling*, an *emotion* that should be used to *guide* people and because love is an emotion, they are then guided by how they *feel*. Since they do not believe in absolutes, then their actions of love stem from how they *feel*, not on what they should do because God has defined love for us.

This is the way it is for those within the New Age. Nothing is really bad or evil, except evil spirits. People, who make bad decisions in this life, will get the chance to correct them in a future, reincarnated life. If someone kills someone else with malice, to those deeply entrenched in New Age thought, the person who was murdered really *wanted* to die. Yes, the killer is still culpable, but in the spirit world, it is viewed differently. Both murderer and murdered are working out their karma. Human life in our bodies becomes valueless.

The saddest part of all of this is that people wind up being tossed to and fro, led one day by this idea or feeling, and the next, led by another feeling. It does not matter because all that really counts is

---

[65] Carol W. Parrish-Harra *Messengers of Hope* (New Age Press, 1983), 14

the *outcome*. As Parrish-Harra stated, the individual is not important at all. What is important then, is humanity as a *unit*.

Valueless

Unfortunately, when this happens, individual human beings lose all value. While God saved man for the pinnacle of His Creation because man was the most important aspect of His Creation, the New Age teaches that this is not the case. God created *one man* and then *one woman*. He did *not* create an entire population or civilization at the same time. He placed great value in the individuality of Adam and then Eve. The New Age teaches otherwise that the individual should give way to the *entirety of humankind*.

This is exactly what Satan wishes to achieve. The more humanity comes to see itself as *one*, the greater Satan will be able to achieve his purposes. Do not misunderstand. Satan does *not* win, but that fact does not keep him from trying. At least in some way, he will *appear* to win part of the battle, because along with him being thrown into the Lake of Fire, millions of human beings will join him there. However, God is victorious and all things that Satan attempts to accomplish *fail*.

If you take the time to consider it, there are numerous types of terrorism alive and well today. We have those who are obviously and outwardly terrorists, who are more than willing to die for the cause and do so, taking innocent people with them. These are the fanatics, who are high on the idea of coming to the defense of Allah in order that they might gain paradise at the precise moment of their 'martyrdom.'

There are other terrorists though, who walk and live among us. They have jobs as we have jobs. They live in a house down the street. They have children and they attend PTA meetings. These terrorists are not so easy to see because outwardly they *look* and *act* as we do, doing all the normal, mundane things that most of us do in life. Then one day, they step out from behind their masquerade and bring death and mayhem down on innocent people around them.

Still other terrorists are working *within* the system to bring changes to the land, changes in the form of new laws, new thought, and new tolerance. One day, we may well wake up to learn that our country now has laws, which make it illegal to carry a Bible in public because that may fall under the lack of intolerance laws. We may find that our laws are being shaped so that they become eerily reminiscent of those laws in other parts of the world where a thief is punished by losing a hand, a liar by losing his tongue, an adulterer y being put to death.

Just as we have human terrorists throughout this world, who do not approach the issue of terror the same way, so too do we have to deal with terrorists in the spiritual realm who approach and attack humanity in various ways. We have the obvious evil spirits who take over a person's body through the process of exorcism. We have other "good" spirits who are benignly referred to as walk-ins, or enlightened beings. The thing that separates them, we are told, is their *intent*. Obviously, evil spirits *intend* to do us harm. It is obvious because of their actions from within the possessed human being. The other spirits - the "good" ones - are here to help us it is claimed. Proof of that is seen in the results of their work in and through people.

Is there a difference though, between the intentions of "evil" and "good" spirits, or are they both cut from the same cloth? Could this be one giant hoax? If so, evil spirits are thought to be evil for the ugliness they create in people, yet the "good" spirits are creating ugliness of a different kind, but from the same source.

Chapter 8
Last Days Are Here

Something is happening in this world that is understood differently by different groups. Though sinister in its origin, most people see it as *heavenly*, *loving*, *light*, and *beautiful*. How can this be that the same thing can be seen in two different ways?

Simply stated, how spiritual things are understood all depends upon a person's perspective and worldview. There must be some authority by which people distinguish between right and wrong and even *how* they determine something to be either right or wrong. When people disagree on *what* is right and wrong, and *how* that is determined, that is where the problems come to the fore. It is obvious that what is happening in the world today is creating a huge gulf between those who are authentic Christians and those who are not. This gulf will continue to increase in size because of the very fact that the New Age movement itself continues to grow with more people adopting many of its ways on a near-daily basis.

New Age Continues to Emerge
When speaking of the New Age, it is important to understand that from this author's perspective, that *includes* the Emergent Church, which is coming to rely more heavily on mysticism to determine "God's will" than the authoritative Word known as the Bible. This is thanks to teachings of heretics like Brian McLaren, Tony Campolo, and others who have not only questioned the veracity of God's Word, but also changed meanings of important sections to mean something they do not mean.

Ultimately, the Emergent Church encourages a feelings-based religion that works itself out attempting to improve the social structure of individual societies and the world. This is juxtaposed against a knowledge-based *relationship* with Jesus Christ stemming from a new birth, or spiritual transaction. From this new birth comes a new way of living, one in which *God* is glorified, not the person.

We need to ask ourselves what, if any difference at all really exists between the Emergent Church and the New Age. Determining that will help us understand more about where this age is heading, at least if the Bible has anything to say about it, and fortunately, it is not silent on the issue.

Within the New Age, just about anything goes, as long as it does not resemble what many see as the intolerance of Christianity. Certainly, it is permissible to discuss and even mention Jesus, but only in terms of His *self-actualization*. This is the point at which He realized that He was already divine, just as we are supposed to come to that same conclusion about ourselves.

Discussing Jesus as God the Son, or the "way, the truth, and the life," creates problems for others because it *imposes* beliefs on others, which of course may make them feel stifled in their own search for self-actualization.

Similarly, in New Age beliefs, Satan is not necessarily a real entity, but a compilation of *ideas* or *spirits* that are evil. These work against humanity to keep us from becoming aware of our own deity. Evil spirits are not evil spirits as the Bible describes them. They are entities from other spheres, planets, or galaxies and as some people are "good," by nature and others "evil," the same applies to these entities we refer to as evil spirits.

Though New Agers would deny that they are Satanists, there are some stark similarities between the two groups. In their book *Satanism*, by Bob and Gretchen Passantino, they define Satanism, as it is understood today. "*Anti-morality is foundational to contemporary satanisn and can be found among various groups in history.*"[66] At once, we can see the connection between New Age and Satanism in that both deny that there are absolutes. Truth, and therefore morality, is relative.

"*'Do What You Will!' is one of the most popular phrases borrowed both by Satanist and by witch and is often erroneously attributed to Aleister Crowley. It actually originated with Rabelais in 1535 as the motto for his imaginary community of sensual delight, Thélème.*"[67]

Essentially, most Satanists reject the view that the God of the Bible exists. For the Satanist, Self is god. The Satanist often considers him

---

[66] Bob and Gretchen Passantino *Satanism* (Zondervan, 1995), 39
[67] Ibid, 39

or her the highest form of human life and that they should be worshipped. Regarding Jesus, he is nothing more than a mythological figure. Many believe that Jesus never really existed.

They regard the idea of Jesus Christ with disdain. *"Who wants to emulate someone who wouldn't defend himself and who preached sentimental 'love' instead of self-defense and personal power?"*[68] Along these lines, though varied in belief and opinion, generally speaking, Satanists view Satan as an impersonal, dark force.

The Passantinos state *"Satanism is the religion of hedonism, or self-indulgence. One could argue with a Satanist that if sin and salvation, heaven and hell do exist, the consistent hedonist has every reason to investigate their reality and determine the best way to avoid sin and hell and the best way to enjoy salvation and heaven."*[69]

Many (including this author) believe that the Last Days are upon us. It is for this reason that things seem to be catapulting this world ahead and breakneck speed. The rise of the New Age movement and the rise of that movement within the visible church (Emergent Church), along with an increasing acceptance of Satanism, Witchcraft, and Goddess Worship are all signs that indicate major upheaval in the spiritual realm.

In 2 Thessalonians 2:6-10, Paul speaks of a Restrainer. There are numerous views regarding the identity of this Restrainer. This author believes that it is none other than the Holy Spirit. It seems that Paul is stating that for *now* the Holy Spirit works to keep back the powers of darkness from completely spilling over onto the earth. One day, He will simply move out of the way *allowing* pure and unadulterated to rush in as water behind a dam when the dam no longer exists.

---

[68] Bob and Gretchen Passantino *Satanism* (Zondervan, 1995), 69
[69] Ibid, 77

"And now ye know what withholdeth that he might be revealed in his time. For the mystery of iniquity doth already work: only he who now letteth will let, until he be taken out of the way. And then shall that Wicked be revealed, whom the Lord shall consume with the spirit of his mouth, and shall destroy with the brightness of his coming: Even him, whose coming is after the working of Satan with all power and signs and lying wonders, And with all deceivableness of unrighteousness in them that perish; because they received not the love of the truth, that they might be saved."

Because the Holy Spirit is standing in the gap so to speak, as much as evil would like to, it cannot get through in its entirety and full ferocity. I believe this is why there have been many unfulfilled prophecies from those within the New Age camp regarding the coming *savior* to mankind. There have also been many messages transmitted to human beings about a coming *evacuation*, which is allegedly designed to remove all of the malcontents from this planet. This in turn, will allow spiritual evolution to take place here, permitting the earth and all remaining citizens to evolve to the next spiritual plane.

In reading many of these prophecies from people like Barbara Marciniak and others, one excuse after another is given by these entities to explain why this evacuation has not yet occurred. The reason always has to do with humanity itself. People have not come together enough, they have not become *one* in thought and belief. They have not rejected antiquated forms of ancient religions (named Christianity), which has cast a hold over the entire earth.

Laying the blame squarely at the feet of human beings, the extraterrestrial entities, or enlightened beings, or whatever someone calls them, are absolved of any responsibility in timing. It is clear that they see things happening in the spiritual realm, because that is where they exist. They witness God's angels going to and fro, and they see what God is doing through His children on this earth, but from that they can only make educated guesses, so they do. When they do not pan out, they simply throw blame for their unfulfilled prophecies in the laps of people.

Intolerance on the Rise
This also serves to create problems for Christians, because as time progresses, we will see more intolerance toward Christians. This will be seen as *correct* and *needed*. It is allegedly the Christian's antiquated views that keep earth from moving to the next spiritual plane. Anger, frustration, and outright hatred will increase against Christians and it will become the accepted norm.

Already we see this slowly, but consistently coming to the fore. It is quickly becoming something that is considered hate-speech when stating that homosexuality is wrong. People in Great Britain have already been jailed for that "offense."

Similarly, Muslims and Islam itself is becoming *more* tolerated, if for no other reason than the fact that people know that they face execution from Islamic jihadists and extremists who are easily offended when it comes to the world's view of Allah or Muhammad. These things and others are gearing up to the boiling point and there will need to be a scapegoat. Just as Nero and other Roman emperors found docile Christians to be the perfect victim in their day, history will likely repeat itself.

Once the Holy Spirit moves aside, permitting hell to empty itself of all evil, vomiting itself onto the land, the landscape will change, *drastically*. It is doubtful that anyone living today has a good mental picture of just how bad things will get, but of course, the Bible provides clues.

With the Holy Spirit stepping aside, and evil streaming in, people will become absolute evil. This is already happening little by little. Paul tells us *"This know also, that in the last days perilous times shall come. For men shall be lovers of their own selves, covetous, boasters, proud, blasphemers, disobedient to parents, unthankful, unholy, Without natu-*

ral affection, trucebreakers, false accusers, incontinent, fierce, despisers of those that are good, Traitors, heady, highminded, lovers of pleasures more than lovers of God; Having a form of godliness, but denying the power thereof: from such turn away. For of this sort are they which creep into houses, and lead captive silly women laden with sins, led away with divers lusts, Ever learning, and never able to come to the knowledge of the truth," (2 Timothy 3:1-7).

If we list the attributes of men in the last days, it looks like this:

- *Lovers of themselves*
- *Covetous*
- *Proud*
- *Braggarts*
- *Blasphemers*
- *Disobedient to parents*
- *Unthankful*
- *Unholy*
- *Without natural affection*
- *Liars*
- *Lacking self-control*
- *Haters of what is good*
- *Traitors*
- *Arrogant*
- *Hedonists*
- *Pretending to be religious*

Now, give some thought to the way people are today. I spent ten years teaching in elementary public schools. If I were to consider the bulleted list and compare it to students, it would be easy to point to many of these bulleted items and apply them to students I personally taught.

Hedonists Gone Wild
Most of us likely know people like this (and before we look too hard at

others, maybe we should take some time to identify any of those traits at work in us). We know people who brag about themselves, who are arrogant, who love themselves more than anything or anyone. We all know of people who seem to have no self-control at all, but do what they want to do.

The attitudes expressed by many today is a rousing cheer of, *"I will do whatever I want, when I want!"* People do not want to be told they cannot do something. They do not want limits placed on them. They do not care if they lie to their neighbor, or if they falsely accuse someone else. If there is something in it for them, it is permissible.

People today are truly hedonists, going from one party to the next, always looking for the next "pleasure fix." Many of these people, to keep up appearances, attend some type of church, and act the part of a Christian while there, but quickly shed that guise in favor of their true and favored guise. However, even authentic, yet immature believers are unfortunately being caught up into this way of thinking and living.

Peter tells us we are to have none of that. *"Wherefore gird up the loins of your mind, be sober, and hope to the end for the grace that is to be brought unto you at the revelation of Jesus Christ; As obedient children, not fashioning yourselves according to the former lusts in your ignorance: But as he which hath called you is holy, so be ye holy in all manner of conversation; Because it is written, Be ye holy; for I am holy.,"* (1 Peter 1:13-16).

Authentic believers are supposed to be the exact opposite of Paul's description of what people will be like in the last days. Self-control is something that few people seem to have these days, yet it is something that is to be one of the hallmarks of the Christian's life.

Peter also seems to echo Paul's thoughts when he says, *"there shall come in the last days scoffers, walking after their own lusts, And saying, Where is the promise of his coming? for since the fathers fell asleep, all things continue as they were from the beginning of the creation. For this they willingly are ignorant of, that by the word of God the heavens were of old, and the earth standing out of the water and in the water: Whereby the world that then was, being overflowed with water, perished: But the heavens and the earth, which are now, by the same word are kept in store, reserved unto fire against the day of judgment and perdition of ungodly men,"* (2 Peter 3:3-7).

Peter describes many people today who scoff at the idea that Jesus will return physically. He also states that these people are *willingly ignorant*, meaning they *want* to believe a lie, as opposed to the truth. They have no clue at all, but they firmly believe they have more than a clue. They believe they have *the* truth. Peter says they not only have nothing, but will be judged harshly for their denial of the absolute truth.

People within the New Age accept lies for truth as the norm. They believe God to be a type of god that incorporates all that is god, while allowing people – human beings – to become the same as that god over time and through many reincarnations.

Within the New Age, there might be Satanists, or adherents of Witchcraft, or neo-paganism, or those who profess Goddess Worship. In essence, these are all part of the same lie, yet because of their differences (minor in some cases), people are free to choose an area that suits them the best.

Witchcraft and Goddess Worship both believe that Mother Earth is alive. Gaia as earth is also known is *feminine*. Adherents invoke goddesses, or *the* goddess to help them achieve and gain what they believe to be their rightful place over men. They believe that if/when this occurs, all will be on its way to becoming right in the world, which has been severely marred by the supremacy of men (in position).

Satan Evangelizes

In truth, it does not matter if it is Satanism, Witchcraft, Goddess Worship, or some other form of Neo-paganism, because the same entity is behind all of them. The greatest expression of all these things is found within the New Age movement. Yes, it keeps coming back to that and for good reason. All things anti-God emanate from that hub.

In their book *Satan's Evangelistic Strategies for This New Age*, Erwin Lutzer and John F. DeVries point out that, *"The New Age Movement is known by various names. Some of the most common designations are the Age of Aquarius, the New Consciousness, the New Orientalism, Cosmic Humanism, the New World Order, the New Esotericism, and the New Globalism. Whatever the name, the basic presuppositions are the same."*[70] The phrase 'new world order' has become common today, constantly on the lips of educators and politicians alike. People are yearning for a time when war will be something of the past, when all people will be treated equally, and when life will be a walk in the park.

The New Age is everywhere as stated; it has most certainly made its way into the visible church. Along with the many names that label it, the New Age movement has numerous signs and logos as well. *"the rainbow, pyramids, concentric circles, rays of light, crystals, and the unicorn are the most popular. Often the number 666 is worked into various diagrams and signs. All of these signify that we are saying farewell to the Piscean Age (the era of Christianity) and welcoming the New Age of Aquarius. We are, according to the New Agers, leaving darkness to enter the era of light."*[71]

This is certainly an interesting way of looking at things, but it should not surprise authentic believers that what they believe is seen as old-fashioned, out of touch with reality, and simply antiquated. It is all

---

[70] Erwin Lutzer and John F. DeVries *Satan's Evangelistic Strategies for This New Age* (Victor Books), 15
[71] Ibid, 15

part of the process Satan uses to capture hearts and minds of people everywhere. From all outward appearances, it is working.

Lutzer and DeVries list seven principles that Satan uses to captivate his unwary audience.[72] These seven concepts make a great deal of sense and when considered, it is realized that this is what marketing is based upon. We will list the principles here and expand on them afterward.

1. *Promise that your techniques bring success*
2. *Mix truth with error*
3. *Sell your product under the guise of science*
4. *Use language to disguise your identity*
5. *Communicate through entertainment*
6. *Stress techniques that glorify self-effort rather than rational religious principles or doctrine*
7. *Counter setbacks with the reminder that we are all in a state of evolutionary transformation*

Stop and consider that most marketing strategies use and apply many or all of these seven principles. Let's expand on these one at a time from their book.

Promise That Your Techniques Bring Success
Most people would like to be financially well off, not having to worry about how to make payments for cars, homes, vacations, and children's education. Because of this, marketing campaigns for products include promises. These promises are geared to the wants and desires of the buying public.

People often set aside good judgment because the promises sound so...*promising*. Most of us believe that companies would not be able

---

[72] Erwin Lutzer and John F. DeVries *Satan's Evangelistic Strategies for This New Age* (Victor Books), 32-46

to make promises unless the promises are true. Therefore, they must work. What is the harm?

In situations where group exercises are led by some leader with a great deal of charisma, the point is to place complete trust in that leader. This causes the individuals in the group to trust him or her completely. This then leads to setting aside good judgment to go along with the group. In the end, people become little more than animatronics robots, dutifully obeying the instructions of the leader.

"Supporters of these human potential seminars are convinced that they have found the secret that can solve the problems of business stagnation. Thus the basic occult dictum that you have all the resources you need within you is finding its way into more and more of the corporate world. This is a new form of spirituality that considers indulgence to be a virtue."[73]

Mix Truth with Error
This is of course where Satan and his subordinates excel. As we have stated before in previous books, Satan will design a method just for each individual. *"If Satan wants to reach those Americans who have no interest in mind-expanding seminars but who are into health food, he will have to design a special program just for them. Remember, there are as many routes to the occult as there are interests among Americans."*[74]

The word "holistic" is big in the health food industry. People want to be "whole" and to arrive at this is not simply a matter of eating correctly. Added to that must be exercise and even the proper way to *think*. People have come to believe that the ability to heal lies in the body and mind. What is needed is the proper frame of mind, the ad-

---
[73] Erwin Lutzer and John F. DeVries *Satan's Evangelistic Strategies for This New Age* (Victor Books), 34
[74] Ibid, 34

dition of certain herbs, and if necessary reflexology or something similar.

When all is said and done though, while it is **true** that most people would benefit greatly by changing their diets and adding exercise to their daily routine, going beyond this into the uncertain area of herbs and other holistic practices is merely another way of adopting occult practices.

The belief that my mind has the power to heal the body is patently *false*. While we all know that a positive attitude can *help*, it will not cure cancer, or AIDS, or other diseases.

Sell Your Product Under the Guise of Science

We see this more and more within the New Age. Even Kryon's discussions about DNA sound scientific and more easily accepted by the masses. Sounding scientific and *being* scientific are two different things altogether. If someone includes science or scientific lingo in their sales pitch, it is difficult to ignore, because most people place such a high degree of confidence in science.

Lutzer and DeVries offer this example of an ad that is touted as being scientific, yet obviously includes Eastern Mysticism:

> **"INTRODUCTORY OFFER...ASTROFLASH**
> **LET THE COMPUTERS AND THE STARS WORK FOR YOU.**
> **MORE THAN A HOROSCOPE...A COMPLETE**
> **ASTROLOGICAL STUDY**
> **DEVELOPED BY WORLD FAMOUS ASTROLOGER**
> **GET THIS $100.00 VALUE FOR ONLY $19.95."**[75]

The authors then conclude that *"This ad guarantees: (1) personal attention, (2) the combination of ancient wisdom and modern technolo-*

---

[75] Erwin Lutzer and John F. DeVries *Satan's Evangelistic Strategies for This New Age* (Victor Books), 37

gy, and (3) the promise of a six-month forecast."[76] The authors also point out that oftentimes, these ads bring fairly accurate results to those who put out the cash for it. The problem of course is that if it *appears* to work the first time, it does so due to demons bringing their own predictions to fruition. Beyond this, once results are seen, it is easy to become addicted to this type of system.

As people place their faith in these idolatrous systems, they wind up involving themselves in occult practices. Once involved in the occult, they are opening the door to demonic entities, who will stop at nothing (short of being exposed and exorcised through the power of Jesus Christ), to gain full control of the individual that has come to depend upon the "power" of these unseen forces.

Use Language to Disguise Your Identity
Authors Lutzer and DeVries point out that the meaning of the word occult is *hidden*. *"For this reason it is always associated with deception. The devil is a master of disguise. He cannot speak plainly, but must always protect his true identity with the cloak of misinformation. The flexibility of language serves him well. It is easier to create new vocabulary than to speak in descriptive terms that people understand."*[77]

This is certainly true! Spend some time reading some of the messages transmitted through humans by these demons. What is seen is language that appears to be English, yet the verbiage is interestingly misleading, yet well placed. Lutzer and DeVries point out that no businessperson would attend a seminar openly stating that it would help people become Hindu. Yet, with another title that simply deals with meditation to become successful in business is an open door. What businessperson would not want to be more successful? Cer-

---

[76] Erwin Lutzer and John F. DeVries *Satan's Evangelistic Strategies for This New Age* (Victor Books), 37
[77] Ibid, 40

tainly, in this way, while most are aware that meditation is a form of religion, since it is presented in a way that is only related to business, the religious aspect of it is not generally seen.

Communicate Through Entertainment
This is a huge one. We are all familiar with the adage; *A picture is worth a thousand words.* A movie, a concert, a song, or something similar all work to create pictures in our mind, and ultimately seek to manipulate our emotions and feelings. Once our feelings and emotions become manipulated by the message, it can and often does become part of our worldview.

Consider George Lucas' Star Wars saga. Who does not feel empathy for Yoda. Our heart naturally goes out to creatures who *appear* to us to be weaker, even though in the movie, Yoda is far stronger than Luke. Star Wars became a mega hit for Lucas literally overnight and the symbolism built into the series of movies has stayed with people since. The Force is composed of two sides, the light, and the dark. Obi Wan was a Jedi Knight on the light (or correct) side of the Force, while Darth Vader, who started out there, moved over to the dark side (or the wrong) of the Force.

Since the Force is completely *impersonal* (and therefore, truth is relative), it is up to each person to decide for himself or herself which side they will choose. Choosing either, according to the movie, has its virtues; it merely depends upon the preference of each individual. Though the entertainment industry started out harmlessly decades ago, it has since grown into something that focuses on horror, Sci-Fi with impersonal forces, and comedy that drags viewers through the sewer.

For those who are unaware, "Hollywood" actually began in New Jersey and the surrounding areas. This is where entertainment in movies started and it grew from there. Shows like "Car 54 Where Are You?" were filmed in Brooklyn, NY. Eventually, weather conditions

Spiritual Terrorism

forced studios to look elsewhere and California seemed to be a good place since sunlight was plentiful. The constant sun allowed for open-roof studios where silent films were shot during the day without having to use heavy, costly lighting systems. Soundstages could literally be open-air, which made it much easier to film as well.

From those early days of screwball comedy and Keystone Cops, the entertainment industry developed into a studio system in which "stars" were contracted to one particular studio. This normally guaranteed them work and the studio always had its bevy of stars to call upon for one movie or the next.

This system finally gave way to the independent studio and independent star. The benefits for those who made it in Hollywood are many. It also opened the door to the independent filmmaker, and because of that, things began heating up, with one indy filmmaker trying to outdo another to gain a favorable market share.

Ever since the studio system went into retirement, it seems as

Splice, ©2010 Warner Bros. Entertainment. All rights reserved.

though everything under the sun has come out to gain notoriety and fame. The more gross the effects, the better. In the old days of movie making, things were left to the imagination. In today's business, guts, blood, and all else is routinely splattered across the screen. Nothing is left to the imagination at all.

A recent movie release called *Splice* is about human-animal hybridization. The question is *why*? Why do we need to experiment with animals and humans? Answer: we do *not*, but will it happen? It could and in this author's mind, it is a throwback to the days of Noah. The main characters in the film take the time to splice together DNA from humans and animals. While they start off splicing DNA from different animals to create to new animal hybrids, they eventually move onto experimentation with human and animals. The initial hybrid creation is a creature they name *Dren*. She exhibits fantastic physical and mental prowess, but eventually becomes the terror they never expected.

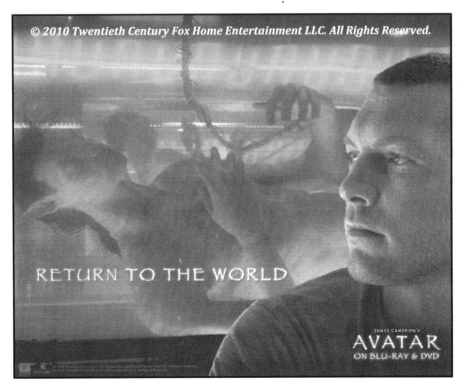

Science has always wanted to create life, from before *Frankenstein* to now. Movies like these indulge the fantasies while at the same time provide a growing interest in the whole area of DNA intermingling.

Another movie that recently became a blockbuster is *Avatar*. This particular movie blends the ancient with the modern. *"When his brother is killed in a robbery, paraplegic Marine Jake Sully decides to take his place in a mission on the distant world of Pandora. There he learns of greedy corporate figurehead Parker Selfridge's intentions of driving off the native humanoid "Na'vi" in order to mine for the precious material scattered throughout their rich woodland. In exchange for the spinal surgery that will fix his legs, Jake gathers intel for the cooperating military unit spearheaded by gung-ho Colonel Quaritch, while simultaneously attempting to infiltrate the Na'vi people with the use of an "avatar" identity. While Jake begins to bond with the native tribe and quickly falls in love with the beautiful alien Neytiri, the restless Colonel moves forward with his ruthless extermination tactics, forcing the soldier to take a stand - and fight back in an epic battle for the fate of Pandora."*[78]

The movie uses a tremendous amount of symbolism and religious beliefs from the Native Americans. Pandora is a planet that is a living soul (Gaia), with the trees that all connect one with another. Through them, they have the power to return life, or even exchange life from one body (human) to another (Na'vi). This is accomplished of course through the proper 'Native American' ritual.

Most know of James Cameron's (director) affinity for the mystical, and his movies have become more heavily reliant upon that medium. In this particular movie, Jake is able to enter into the body of his 'avatar' through a special machine that transports his own mind and soul into it. While in the machine, he *is* his avatar. The avatars are roughly 8 to 10 feet tall and have tremendous physical abilities.

---

[78] http://www.imdb.com/title/tt0499549/plotsummary

This type of movie is becoming the norm because of the rise of mysticism in all areas of our global society. Mysticism is hugely popular and through the venue of films, has made a great impact on society, and gained many new followers because of it.

Stress Techniques That Glorify Self-Effort
It really should go without saying that for those caught up in the human potential seminars, the books, the movies, and other forms of media, the emphasis is on self's ability to achieve whatever the person dreams or thinks.

Authors Lutzer and DeVries rightly point out that though this has been relatively easy throughout many parts of the world, but not the United States. *"The difficulty Satan has in the United States is that we have had a Christian heritage, a residue of which is still left on our culture. Since this stands in the way of accepting Eastern thought, there is only one way to overcome this hurdle: it is to say that one can still be a Christian and accept New Age through too."*[79] Enter the Emergent Church.

In order for people in America to begin to accept aspects of the Emergent Church into their own daily thinking and living, they must of necessity set aside *moral absolutes*. We can no longer think in terms of something as being right or wrong. We must learn to conclude that while something might be right for one person, it may well be wrong for another, and vice versa.

In this regard, Jesus quickly becomes lowered in status as merely one among *many* saviors, or enlightened ones, or ascended masters. To many within the New Age that thinking has found its way into the visible church. Jesus is no longer God the Son, but simply *a son of God*, which we all have the potential of becoming.

---

[79] Erwin Lutzer and John F. DeVries *Satan's Evangelistic Strategies for This New Age* (Victor Books), 44

The only thing that is not tolerated within both the New Age movement and the Emergent Church is the belief that Jesus is the only way to salvation. Other than this, you are welcome to talk about Jesus, but do not make the mistake of deigning to confess that He is God or as He Himself stated in John 14:6, the way, the truth and the life. By making these claims, the authentic believer becomes the intolerant one, unable to set themselves free from the antiquated, superstitious beliefs of long ago.

Counter Setbacks with the Reminder That We Are All In a State of Evolutionary Transformation

Science is good at this. Though they have been completely unable to prove beyond doubt how life began on this planet, all science has to do is say "We do not have the answer...yet" and everyone who adores science is satisfied. Yet, when a Christian is unable to fully explain how God could be three-in-one, they are shouted down, castigated, and denigrated for believing some myth that they are unable to fully explain.

It is extraordinarily easy within the New Age to continually point to the fact that as human beings who are gods, and therefore, we are always developing. There will be setbacks, frustrations, and times of trouble, but these are merely steps to the final realization of our inner godhood. We must persevere in our own self-efforts to actualize and release our deity. Let nothing stand in our way.

Like the butterfly, which transforms into that creature, it starts as a caterpillar. The transformation takes time and it is fraught with potential dangers. We must patiently persist in allowing and helping our transformation to become complete. Whether they believe so or not, most New Agers see the rest of us as completely *unenlightened*. They pity us, believing firmly that we are still tied to the old, worn out values of absolute right and wrong. They wish they could get us to understand that once we move past these harbingers of death, we will truly learn the value of freedom!

It is clear that *"running throughout these seven principles is the basic lie: you are God, and therefore you deserve the best. Look out for Number One."*[80]

All of these things signal that the end is coming, because all of them create a deep sense of apostasy among those who attend a church. Yet they profess Christianity, but ultimately do not *know* God at all.

In Romans 8, Paul tells us that God *knew* us before the foundations of the earth. The idea here is that God literally had a relationship with us before He created the earth itself, and long before we were ever born on this planet. In other words, God knew us intimately (those who become His children through salvation in Christ), as we know our spouse or a lifelong friend. This intimacy from God assures us that we are His and that He had set us apart from *before* the foundations of this world.

We know that not all who attend church, or who profess Christianity are true believers. We may not know who the tares among the wheat are, but God knows. Those He *foreknew*, He called. Those He called, He justified, and those He justified, He glorified.

God's plan for us existed before He entered into any part of Creation. Since He knew us from eternity past, it makes Jesus' statement *"Depart from me. I never knew you!"* that much more profound. It is as if Jesus is not only saying that He never knew us in *this* life as we lived our life on planet earth, but He never, *ever* knew us even from eternity past!

---

[80] Erwin Lutzer and John F. DeVries *Satan's Evangelistic Strategies for This New Age* (Victor Books), 45

Spiritual Terrorism

Chapter 9
Behind the Veil

We have seen the various techniques that Satan and his crew use to establish their presence in our lives and even in our bodies. We have become so concerned about *external* terrorism from the Middle East and elsewhere that many of us have lost sight of the *real* terrorism, which exists in the spiritual realm.

Around the globe, people strap bombs onto themselves and blow up innocent people along with themselves. In other areas, rockets are shot off into neighboring countries. In this country of the United States, since 9/11, there have been numerous attempts by terrorists to disrupt and destroy. Thousands have lost their lives to terrorists worldwide.

They Wish to Harvest Souls
However, this is nothing compared to the spiritual harvesting of souls by terrorists from the spiritual realm. The Bible says that we should not fear the person who kill the body, but the One who can kill the soul (cf. Matthew 10:28).

If we could see behind the veil that separates the spiritual realm from our realm, most would undoubtedly be frightened indeed. To find out that the 'messengers' you always thought to be fully philanthropic and compassionate turned out to be nothing more than a gaggle of evil, hateful demons disguising themselves as ascended masters would not only take all the air out of your sails and soul, but your heart would likely stop beating because of the fear.

This world is headed on a collision course with God and God *is* the Victor. He is and will manifest Himself in all of His supremacy and sovereignty. No powers of darkness can stop that from happening.

Though defeated, the minions of evil seek to overcome earth's humanity by lying to us, pretending to be something they are not. Is this not what many human terrorists do in order to accomplish *their* goals? It would not work for a terrorist who was planning on blowing himself up in a market square announce it ahead of time, or enter the market area wearing a sign that said *"Death to Infidels! Your Death is Now!"* A human terrorist uses deception to accomplish his goals and he learned it from his master of deception, Satan.

Satan will not stop his efforts until God puts a final end to them. Until that time, he roams around seeking whom he may devour and just because he *can* be as a lion, it does not mean that he *will* reveal himself as one.

Today is the day for salvation. Today is the day that people need to do what they can to protect themselves from the terrorists in the spiritual realm. This can only happen when our lives are safely hidden in Christ (cf. Colossians 3:1-4). Our lives can only be hidden in Christ when we receive the new birth He talked about with Nicodemus. Without the new birth (or spiritual transaction), a person can do whatever they want that they think makes them a Christian, but without this first step, it means nothing.

Becoming a Christian means believing a number of things wholeheartedly:

- *Jesus is who He says He is – God in human flesh*
- *Jesus was born into this world through a virgin*
- *Jesus lived among the people of this world and never once sinned*
- *Because of the perfection of His life, He became a perfect atonement for the sins of the world*
- *Because of His perfection, His bloody death was a pleasing and acceptable sacrifice to God*
- *After three days of being in the grave, He rose from the dead because the grave could not hold Him*

Jesus is God. Jesus died to save you. Jesus rose again and is currently at the right hand of the Father in heaven. Do you believe this? If you fail to believe these points, you cannot be a Christian, no matter what else you do. If you *want* to believe these things but have difficulty, then *pray* to God for His enlightenment, His strength, His ability to see the truth, along with His ability to embrace the truth.

Once this new life occurs within you, you will never be the same. You will come to realize that it is not through self-effort that eternal life is gained, it is through Jesus' efforts on Calvary's cross. Once we come to terms with the fact that we can do nothing to save ourselves, it is then that we begin to realize that if we cannot save ourselves, who can? Only at that point will we realize that Jesus Christ came, lived, and died so that we might have eternal life.

Do you want eternal life? Do you prefer to continue doing what you can to try in vain to earn your way into your perception of heaven? I tell you that you cannot earn your way there. It is a free gift and it is yours for the receiving. Please, *please* receive His salvation today. Speak to the God of the universe. He is far from an impersonal force. He is a real, personal Being who knows you inside and out.

Let Him speak to you. Allow Him to open your eyes to the truth about Jesus Christ. Permit Him to show you what you need and how to receive it.

Please pray to Him today. Receive the only salvation that is available to humanity, the salvation He made possible for you.

Spiritual Terrorism

More Books by Fred DeRuvo

www.studygrowknow.com or wherever quality books are sold!